Black Rose

Empowering the inner Goddess

S'Roya Rose

3RD EYE PUBLICATIONS

BLACKROSE Empowering the GODDESS
Copyright © 2012 by S'Roya Rose
First Limited Edition Printed February 2012
Revised Edition Printed May 2014
ISBN 978 0 9923123 6 7

All rights are reserved...
Other than for personal use. No part of this oracle or guidebook may be reproduced by any mechanical means, photographic, or electronic process, or in the form of a phonographic recording nor may it be stored in a retrieval system, transmitted, or otherwise be copied for public or private use - other than for "fair use" as brief quotations embodied in articles and reviews giving credit to the author S'Roya Rose without prior written permission of the author or publisher. The intent of the author is only to offer information of a general nature to help you in your quest for emotional and spiritual well-being. In the event you use any of the information in this book for yourself, which is your constitutional right, the author and the publisher assume no responsibility for your actions.

BLACKROSE Empowering the inner Goddess, and
The Goddess Oracle card artwork & interpretations
were created, designed and written by S'Roya Rose.
Edited & produced by 3rd Eye Publications.
Images supplied by Shutterstock, iStock & 123rf.

DISTRIBUTED BY PHEONIX DISTRIBUTION:
3 CUMBERLAND DRIVE, SEAFORD. VICTORIA 3198. AUSTRALIA
PH: 03 8765 8300   FAX: 03 9776 4139

...my dedication
S'Roya

my journey to the Goddess...

My journey to the Goddess began in my early 20's as a natural organic awakening process as I quested for answers spiritually. My mothers illness was to be the catalyst for us both as we began to learn about metaphysical healing, and energy through the understanding of Reiki. It was a magical time that saw us one at a time become Reiki Master Teachers. Having taught Reiki and healing for a few years, I began to run regular empowering 'SacredWomen's days' at my home in the mountains Sunshine Coast, QLD. This was to be the start of truly awakening my inner Goddess/Priestess connection. I was always drawn to all things magical and spiritual, being a natural eclectic mystic. I would always honour the seasons and different spirit realms with offerings and blessings as I came to know each of them. Years later after having written my first two books, and third marriage break up, returning back from New Zealand, I began an open Sacred Women's Circle in Brisbane holding regular Full Moon path working rituals - I was now in my mid 40s. However, it was through my business 'Harmony House Psychic Tea Rooms' which I began in Paddington Brisbane, that I met a Sister Goddess, who after showing her my two magazine ideas, became my business partner in publishing two national Goddess Magazine's. BlackRose & Goddess magazine's were famous regarding the Sacred Feminine, having creating a huge awakening and shift with in Australian women and men alike. It was to be a very powerful time for us both as the Goddess worked her magic. Alas the business partnership dissolved some 18 months later, however I was guided to keep the Goddess energy flowing regardless, so re-created 'Goddess Guru Ezine' making it free online magazine. Since then I've created my Modern Goddess Oracle cards, my S'Roya Rose TAROT deck, my Blue Moon Oracle wisdom cards and written numerous other metaphysical books, a new journey had begun.

A few years ago if you had told me I would take a two-week trip to the UK, visit a little village called Glastonbury, and wind up feeling happier and more content and at home than anywhere else in the world, I would not have believed you. At 49 years old, having spent most of my life living in Australia, I discovered this historic place was my soul's true spiritual home. And it's obvious to me now that the goddess had always been there, silently urging me on, beckoning me back to her, long before I even remembered who she was. It's a strange thing when you're faced with this kind of inner truth. My Goddess heart had come home to Avalon - one of it's ancient priestesses returned. She was so familiar to me. I felt so calm that a sense of inner peace came over me, that only a soul at home would understand. I sang in the Glory of it all...

We all come from the goddess and to her we will return, like a drop of rain running to the ocean...

I have heard the call of the goddesses and sorceresses for many years and I have been dedicated to her as a practicing priestess for some time. Having run Full Moon open sacred women's circles, for path-working women in Queensland for many years, long before I ever published magazines. I held Sacred Women's days up in the mountains behind the Sunshine Coast, where we painted our breasts and did sacred aboriginal dances and learnt ceremonies to honour the earth in the 90's. I had already dutifully embraced my healing gifts and energetic shamanic medicines as they were each presented, as I walked the path of the goddess once again. I was put through numerous shamanic deaths, I shed many worn out life skins, was stripped of all my earthly possessions and partners more than once. I eventually started speaking in my cosmic star language, using the spirit tones/sounds that my voice was gifted to heal the fractured feminine souls of others. I had walked alone on my journey, been shed of my ego and wept more tears than I care to remember, all to embrace my soul and become a living goddess once again.

Nothing can truly prepare you for this kind of transformational life journey. I bare the scars of a well travelled goddess who has been put to task to reclaim her powers, and I can identify with others who have gone before me on this sacred journey. I went through much of it kicking and screaming, resisting it all in the beginning – as the overwhelming sense of having to let go control of everything - including my mind – frightened me. But once I stopped resisting and surrendered to her call, I was able to embrace many gifts. I embraced my psychic abilities in full force and made contact with many spirit guides, angels and beings from other realms and dimensions.

I travelled through inter-dimensional doorways via numerous portals and visited other worlds and realities. I got to cosmically connect with the outer realms and with inner realms of the mind. I learned that I could retrieve information from places that just astounded me as a psychic and oracle. I could see into time and go beyond my mind and learned to trust all my clairvoyance visions and clairsentient feelings and once honed they became like cats whiskers - able to detect even the slightest changes and subtleness of energies. I then learned to trust all that was given to me and never doubted the guidance that walked by my side. There were times my faith was tested but I never failed to stay on track. I faced many challenging spiritual experiences that scared me witless. I faced my inner fears and demons and made great personal sacrifices to be true to my soul's chosen path. I lost lovers, husbands, family alliances and friends to be true to who I am today. Had I known how difficult this was going to be in advance, I might never have undertaken such an intense journey. My soul had done this before, it was all too familiar.

The goddess is in everything – she's in nature, the cosmos, the universe and she does not judge or take sides, she simply holds everything in balance.

Now I was delivered into the sacred bosom of Avalon, suckling on her like a new birthed child - hungry for the Goddesses life giving essence, knowing that it sustains the very core of my being. The energy of the goddess is everywhere and can be felt, seen and heard here. Avalon's energy holds the true heart of the goddess; you can feel her nurturing essence washing over you like a gentle soft babbling brook on a summer's day. She is life giving in a way that words cannot express. She can be seen in the shops, in the eyes of those walking down the street, in the food that is prepared, in the way one feels walking on the land. I am still alone but I am full with the mother goddess and need nothing else to sustain me. I am always excited at meeting and connecting with like minded others whose lives have been transformed by a similar inner journey.

As goddesses converge into Avalon, for all the right reasons, (the annual goddess conference put on by Kathy Jones and her Melissa's was fast approaching) I met many from all over the globe, while just sitting having coffee in a local café. We shared our spiritual journeys, swapped our life stories, we poured ourselves out to each other like long lost sisters. It was intoxicating and fed me in a way I've not felt for a long time.

Old Magic in a New Age

Many of the old magical practices are visiting a revival, as the goddesses reclaim their dormant ancient sacred knowledge once again. Rituals and ceremonies are rejoiced and encouraged as being normal practice here in Avalon. The initiations I have received so far have been direct from spirit. The Lady of the Lake visited me one night at three am. She was standing majestically on her huge carved boat as it came sailing through my bedroom at a local bed and breakfast at the base of the Tor. I was robed and crowned, given a sceptre, welcomed back as a high priestess of Avalon and asked to take my rightful place again and dedicate my life to the goddess (like I hadn't already). Then I was taken through the great rite and married to the horned god once again. This was for balancing my polarity, bringing wholeness and balance so as to embrace the true love of an equal soul mate once again. I saw numerous gods and goddesses who were all there to celebrate my return. Now years ago I would have thought all this stuff kind of loopy, but now it all seems common place, like an everyday spiritual event to me.

These kinds of spiritual initiations are common for those of us used to dealing with the realms of spirit, awakening aspects of our deeper selves long forgotten. I must admit to taking them in my stride as normal these days, but there once was a time I didn't. I have realised that my connection to the goddess goes back throughout time and that this is when one embraces the knowledge available from the past in the now. My initiation was a message for my DNA to upload all that has been kept secret within my spiritual archives and deeper Soul memory making it available for my now mind to use again in this life. There is always an integration and assimilation period that takes place after such an intense initiation. I needed to rest, take a bath and allow myself to become known to myself, as I would never be the same again.

Needless to say this High Priestess was getting ready to perform some personal rituals and couldn't wait to dance under the moonlight in the sacred stone circles once again.

In this book and the following chapters I share the essence of the Goddess, her true nature, how you can re-awaken and connect with her within yourself. My hope is you are inspired to do just that, and I would love for you to drop me an email with your comments as to your own journeys. Our world is in dire need of the Goddess returned, may she be reborn within you, so that her strength may heal and remind our global communities, that we are all of her and must respect her, especially in nature as we heal the damage that has been done to our loving mother earth.

I bless each and every one of you and give thanks for your return to the bosom of the Goddess... Blessings)O(

Part One
Awakening to the Goddess

The Goddess is a presence ...
Not a new age ideal or a force!

The term Goddess is mainly used to describe the sacred aspect of woman for she is the divine feminine! She lives and dwells in the ancient heart of all mankind.

Her greatest inner strength lies in her open heart's ability to be vulnerable in love, to love deeply, completely and unashamedly. She lives in our bones as the earth; in our blood as our water; in our mind as the air; in our actions as our fire; in our hearts as true spirit. In awakening her and claiming this aspect of ourselves we can begin to recognize her archetypal strengths and weaknesses within our own character.

Giving us a better understanding of the essence of our inner self and our cosmic link to the collective unconscious. As God is everywhere, so too is the Goddess. She lives in all things and co-creates alongside the God. Awakening both the divine male and female aspects of us is spiritually required for us to become whole in one's self. This is the reason to awaken and claim her natural power!

A Goddess is in touch with herself, mind, body, emotions and spirit!

A modern Goddess is a woman whole in all her female power, comfortable and unafraid of who she is on any level. She is in touch with the very core of herself, able to be raw, intimate, wild and untamed yet equally able to be caring, loving, kind, empathic and compassionate. She is dynamic in her power unable to be owned by anything or anyone! She is a connoisseur of beauty and believes in personal luxury, surrounding herself with the things that bring her joy and pleasure.

Her greatest gifts being her self-realization, her intuitiveness, her natural forgiveness, her inner beauty and total compassion.

She has a natural inner calm, almost regal presence, as her character displays elegance with power and grace. She often commands an audience just by walking through a door, for she rarely goes unnoticed. We affectionately call this the 'Wow' factor.

Like a well-designed quality diamond, she has many amazing facets. She believes in being attractive, which is obvious by the way she looks after herself with pride and presents herself with style no matter what her physical age (often looking younger than her years). She follows her purpose with passion and chooses to be successful in her career. The Goddess in her believes in displaying happiness, wisdom, kindness and love constantly with dignity, fun and often laughter. You feel uplifted when you have been in her presence for she adds to your life.

Her values lie in being real, sensitive, authentic, wise and truthful. The totality of her emotional being relies on living honestly in any moment. This is her quiet power!

In early mythology the Goddess was considered sacred, she was revered and worshipped as the true life giver that nourished mankind's existence. She was seen as the earth, the moon and the stars that held the mystery of the beginning of timeless existence. A mystery that was accepted even though not fully understood. Everything came from her and everything returned to her, the cycles of life were where she reined. Her cosmic, mythic presence constantly echoed her fluidity throughout time and space as the cycles of death and rebirth, the seasons of nature and the rhythms of the universe. She was valued for her mystery and her intuitive innate wisdom was sort after. It was man's need to understand her natural mysteries that gave birth to the original sciences.

Why would I want to awaken her and how would this benefit me in my life now?

For far too long the true essence of the Goddess has been suppressed, not allowed, made to feel wrong, covered up and even banished. Even today there are those who feel quite threatened by women in their true power, especially when they are unable to be controlled or made submissive to other's needs. Bringing equality into our society for women has certainly had its struggles. Unfortunately even though it has improved over the centuries and especially the last 50 years, it is still by no means equal.

Her once inspiring lunar powers are almost unrecognized as valid. Is it any wonder that many sophisticated and accomplished women are mourning the loss of her richness and vitality, feeling empty and betrayed? The Goddess within is being ignored as women's roles are now measured by their accomplishments. She has become veiled by the times, tied to her daily schedules and deadlines, social pressures, honoured for her successful career and academic achievements. Falsely lured by consumerism, convenience, compromise and competition, her inner nature has been deceived. Constantly juggling motherhood, career, love life and family, her desires to look after her loved ones are now cloaked by commercialism and used against her.

The goddess, it seems, is everywhere in chains, visiting therapists, needing help, looking for herself, performing as if she isn't menstruating or pregnant. Her cycles that were once natural rhythms of life are now being diagnosed as medical conditions that need controlling and treating, everything from menstruation to birth control, childbirth to menopause, apparently needing drugs! Her natural aging process is no longer respected and has created insecurities, plagued by youth obsessed media and advertising. She's fixated on having face-lifts, breast implants, lipo suction, and plastic surgery to keep up appearances. To fit in with modern men's sexual ideals, women aren't just having Brazilians; they are actually having nip and tuck labia surgery to trim their girly parts for a neater appearance, making for easier and smoother male sexual entry into their bodies.

We have come from the renaissance where paintings of women's rounded hips, large bosoms, bottoms and tummies were revered, where cellulite was considered normal and womanly. Now we look at flat chested, anorexic looking, girl-child waifs in photography for today's fashion. We have gone from the ridiculous to the sublime ignoring our divinity as goddesses, betraying our inherent nature with superficiality that doesn't serve or honour our truth as an evolving female species.

No wonder women are running off seeking therapy, popping Prozac, having nips and tucks, feeling inadequate. She has been waxed, capillarized, plasticized, sanitized, controlled and manipulated, estranged from her natural cyclic truths. Forsaken dignity and ignored divinity has now developed into insecurity and alienation within many women. Loss of the divine Goddess has created a baron wasteland full of impoverished feminine spirit. Feeling lost and depressed, trying to fit in, to be loved, needing to be perfect, wanting to cope and compete in a male orientated world, who's respect for her natural mysteries and rhythms has all but evaporated.

The *Goddess* is in flow with herself, her rhythms, and her moods, her seasons. Like nature she feels the subtle ebb and flow of life, within and without.

All women have the potential to step into the cosmic Goddess and awaken and unleash her sacred power.

The Goddess as the divine aspect of the Sacred Feminine traditionally has three parts to her natural journey as a woman; the Maiden or youth, a nubile young woman usually (under the age of 21) before she marries or bears a child; the Mother, glowing and fertile nurturer, usually (22-42) once one has married and born children; the Wise One or Dark Goddess usually (43 and older) a mature wiser woman often a grandmother (traditionally she was no longer menstruating). However, there is much more to this original journey than just these three social archetypal aspects.

The divine feminine lives within men and women alike and both can embrace the energy of her as part of their natural duality and total spiritual balance. The Goddess lies dormant, hidden deep within the lunar/moon DNA part of the ancient self, deep within the core or essence of one's Soul. Everyone's Soul has this within his or her cellular memory; we are all born with it.

The goddess is an inherent part of our nature. She naturally surfaces from within our heart and is awakened slowly and subtly as we journey through life. However she is often unnoticed.

If we look for her and embrace her, we can use her natural dormant powers to evolve and become more whole. She lifts the veils of untruths from our heart and offers us clarity and natural wisdom, which aids our integrity adding depth to our being more authentic. Her cosmic energy helps shift our perceptions beyond our linear time concepts to the possibility of other dimensions existing simultaneously.

The Goddess embodies all that is natural, all that is infinite wisdom, all that is infinite love and all that is healing. She is all compassion, all that is intimate, sensual and sexual, all that is beauty, all that represents the essence of the Sacred Feminine. Therefore she is all accepting, all allowing, all that brings balance, and all that is non judgmental and wise. She is the keeper of duality, the very womb of creation, the earth and cosmos combined.

There are many time honoured ways that enable us to get in touch with the many aspects of the Goddess, connecting with her subtle sacredness, helping to awaken the divine feminine part of self.

She understands the natural cycles of life!

To awaken the Goddess within, one must become familiar and in touch with all aspects of one's self.

One must awaken the feminine creative/intuitive/psychic - *mind*; the life bringer/sensual/sexual - *body*; one's moods/inner tides/natural rhythm/ebb and flow - *emotions*; the greatness of one's own active energy/spirit - *soul*.

A Goddess must know herself on all levels within and without. To do this, she must claim all that was once separate, all that was once scattered. She must heal her karmic wounds and gather herself from all that would claim power over her. She must come to know her own heart and mind, to know what serves her and what doesn't, to know what to let go of and what to keep.

She must become emotionally intelligent and wise and learn how to feel safe expressing herself, especially her doubts, fears, anxieties, anger and rage. This is no easy task to undertake and some would say that it is not for the faint hearted. Once known, she is expressed as being a whole woman who is comfortable and at ease with whom she has become - mind, body and spirit.

One must claim all aspects of one's self, including one's duality - the male and female aspects, and one's positive-light along with one's negative-dark aspects.

The Goddess is dormant in every human being, waiting to be awakened then invited to participate in the dance of life, allowed and unleashed and not just in women. There are some men who learn to access and claim their goddess aspect helping to bring about balance to their maleness and duality. It is honoured within men as it is within women. We all have the Goddess aspect within us to a lesser or greater degree. Connecting and embracing the Goddess within will help to create better balance within mankind once again, another reason for us all to awaken and embrace her quiet powers!

Practical tips on connecting with your Inner Goddess!

1. Connect often with Nature.

Walk in her forests and along her shores, marvel at her power in Nature. Feel her ebb and flow, feel her winds and enjoy her skies. Grow flowers, food or herbs and become one with living growing entities. There is something quite marvelous about growing things that gives pleasure and satisfaction on a deep, inner, primal level.

2. Enjoy the company of pets.

Feel the joy of playing with and looking after another living being that loves unconditionally, who gives love back to you. Taking care of them develops real-time responsibility. Coming home to a purring kitten or a wagging tail is great for the moral. On the list of what makes women happy, pets rated number one!

3. Learn to ingest great food and enjoy the creative art of cooking.

Food is an earthly passion, one of life's basic pleasures. Have fun cooking for friends and family is a natural thing for the Goddess to do, for it's all about nurturing. It brings the Goddess great joy and purpose to look after and feed those she loves with healthy home cooked food. Done with purpose and passion often you'll enjoy one of lifes simple goddess pleasures.

4. Enjoy your beauty.

Allow yourself to play with looking and feeling more beautiful. Experiment and fall in love with yourself and your natural beauty, everyone has their own brand of beauty. Have manicures and pedicures, put pretty colours on and enjoy being pretty and girly and beautiful. Indulge in some bling!

5. Pamper your self and learn to let go, receive and relax.

Take time out and have regular spa days. Receive head to toe pampering with facials, pedicures or body massages, they help you to connect with yourself in a very profound way. Besides making you look and feel great they help you to stay balanced, while uplifting your self esteem. Stay in touch with yourself through taking personal time just for you. You deserve it!

6. Allow your emotions to be just as they are.

Get in touch with how you FEEL! Don't be afraid to feel your feelings. This is the first place to start to set yourself free emotionally. Stop bottling pent up emotion, let them out regularly. If you have difficulty try massage and Reiki as a means to gently access your feelings. Try to observe them, instead of judging them.

7. Learn to set boundaries and say "NO".

Claim back your power by setting some healthy boundaries in ALL areas of your life. It's okay; you don't have to be everything to everyone. So set some very well deserved healthy boundaries that serve you too! Ask yourself 'does this serve me too?' If the answer is no then don't say yes to it!

8. Join some self-awareness groups or classes, take up Palates, Chi Gong, Yoga or Tai chi for fun.

Spend time in self-realization and allow for inner growth to become important to you. Become comfortable with your strengths and support your perceived weaknesses as you make adjustments and inner changes. Get inspired, read some personal development or self help books! Take up a class or workshop or two. Be patient with your self as you grow and learn.

9. Place symbolic quiet reminders of the Goddess around where you work and live.

Simple goddess symbols like a vase of flowers, water features and fountains, seashells and plants, crystals and feathers, candles and statues of Venus, or

QuanYin (which are very are popular) or pictures of any other archetypal goddesses you like, help to remind you that you too, are a Goddess.

10. Become aware of how a person or place 'feels' energetically.

You do this by recognizing how it affects you. You have to tune into the subtlety of how you feel about it. Some people and places feel very clam and peaceful while others feel heavy or scattered. Learn to observe the difference in the energies so you can begin to re-create around you what you would rather be feeling.

11. Bask in the moonlight and enjoy her radiance.

Take regular moon baths by sitting outside and looking into her soft evening glow. Let her moonbeams rain down on your face as you connect with their subtle power. Sit on the beach at night and let her silvery light dancing on the water captivate you. Let the experience with her be magical and enchanting. Marvel at her dynamic cycles from full to waning to new moon, to waxing to full again. Dance often outside under her glow, enjoy!

12. Embrace your sensuality.

Feel the joy of having your skin draped in sensual satins and soft lacey tops. Indulge in some beautiful sexy underwear, and don't be afraid to subtly flaunt your curves or cleavage. It will drive men wild and help to lift your confidence if you feel you look sassy and sexy! Fall in love with your sensual nature, use soft pastels to uplift your lips or dynamic red if you feel daring.

13. Set up a Goddess Alter.

Setting up a Goddess Alter acts a focus for attracting her energies to you. You might like to create one for every season as it approaches. Experiment with Full moon alters, chakra alters for healing or Solstices and Equinox's for pathworking. You will need a special place, either a shelf, table or cabinet top or hall stand. Place unique items that are intune with your chosen theme and dedicate it to the Goddess in you. Keep any flowers fresh and clear them regularly. The use of candles, bells, statues and incense are all part of the ritual of keeping a Goddess alter. Enjoy!

Honouring The Goddess & her Sacredness

There is a call from the depth of Womankind to move forward into balance, into honouring her divine feminine soul, enabling her to fully explore the Power of the Goddess.

From the boardroom to the bedroom, from the nursery to the grave, her sacredness must be restored, as the earth and our very survival depends upon it.

To completely honour her and restore her sacredness she has to move away from old energies that no longer serve her. She must shed the skins of the past and heal the old karmic patterns that have forsaken and dishonored her. She must bravely and boldly confront the wounds of humanity that outmoded Patriarchal energies have unfortunately help to create. Within these deep wounds lies the dormant medicine that only her sacred love can use to heal.

As more women the world over search for 'inner balance and harmony', honouring their divinity and seeking refuge with the Goddess once again, they must seek the 'right way' to use this harmony within their lives. This organic process has been an unsettling time for us all, as we stand on the precipice of change. Awkward as moving away from these known masculine energies is, they are the inner challenges we all must face to become whole as a people.

*...When I speak of **Patriarchy**... I speak of the fragmented-**masculine** limited worldview, that still uses control and violence to uphold its need for **dominance**. We have inherited this system; it is not of us or of the men of today, even if some of them use its energy to get their own way.*

Women have been trying to heal this within themselves and their male counterparts for some time. Many women have struggled with repression of one sort or another, fed up with the same old, same old, have rebelled and reluctantly torn themselves away from these controlling ways. Women don't want to resort to the energy of aggression to achieve balance or change, we prefer to serve by exploring new ways to create balance through loving communication.

I've found that many won't even talk about this subject and its faults, it's often too uncomfortable acknowledging its overwhelming presence in our lives, never mind daring to speak about its effect on womankind and how that is perceived. How do you negotiate, resolve or change something of this nature, something so ingrained within the DNA of all mankind, with all its historical bias, and ancient religions to back it up? Sadly it's easy to observe its indoctrination within humanity but is especially obvious within marriage, the 'sacred relationship'. Like David fighting Goliath, women can often feel alienated in the process of challenging it, individually and collectively. But challenge it women must!

As a therapist I've witnessed many unhappy wounded relationships, each person struggling for power or control, needing to be right, needing to be heard, wanting the pain, sorrow and misgivings to be resolved, desperately seeking the road back to love. I found it was the silent unspoken inner truths of women that were the hardest to uncover and to be spoken, which made the greatest difference to their men. I asked myself many times what the right balance between the Masculine and Feminine is, how do we move on from Man versus Woman, to a balanced Yin and Yang? How does LOVE honour and accomplish equality?

Women have learnt to over-ride and even dismiss it within their relationships. However, in her silent unspoken dismissal, she inadvertently agrees. Agreement by omission is common for women; we've learned not to speak up. We feel okay about it, because it allows us to resent the dominance of masculine power, blaming 'their arrogance'. Women have been made feel invisible by it, not important and powerless, adding to the mentality of subservience and victim hood, creating division within relationships. There is obviously no sustainability within this format in any relationship. How can men know how this 'power over' behavior affects us if we are not prepared to explain it to them, to teach them?

We have all been controlled, spoken over, interrupted, dismissed, excused, and dominated to some degree!

How many of you have actually said to a man when this happens "actually that was not nice, in fact it was rude and not supportive of me as a woman"?

How many of you went along with things because it was easier to keep the peace and to just get along, than to stand in your power and speak your truth? This energy uses dominance to silence women. The fear of confrontation or brutality, ridicule and bias stops many from speaking their truths. It has become the accepted norm made light in comedy. Sadly it is a sensitive issue in our society, so speaking out against it has obvious bias and implications, as many women pioneering the way will tell you. It means we have to challenge it at the very core, the place it exists within our individual lives, and that's just what women have been doing, albeit unconsciously worldwide. It's been a silent inner war for her.

Women have been challenging the status quo for some time seeking to bring about balance. This has been especially reflected in the area of relationships, and can be easily seen with the rise in divorce over the last 25 years. There are more single parent families now than ever before. The happy outcome of this tragedy is the newer more balanced generation of young males who have learned to honour the feminine from single mothers raising families on their own. This generation has seen what their forebears did not. They saw how their mothers struggled and sought a different way. Now, there are a few of us who see and understand that we are standing on the threshold of a new consciousness, with all manner of possibilities available for us to choose. Women actually know that these old ways no longer serve either men or women, in fact quite the opposite, they undermine both sexes and have brought us all to a place of massive imbalance, to a point of destruction - an interesting dichotomy as it's also the point of resurrection. Now we have an opportunity for transformation to occur on mass. These are hard truths for many to face, especially given that it dives head on into our 'gender issues' already full of many 'man-woman' type 'sensitive truths'. So how do we honour ourselves as women, how do we go about creating change, without war, without fighting, without aggression, or constantly being caught up in debating who's right or who's wrong?

Speak your Truth.

We need to stop denying and silently ignoring the ongoing undermining of our sex. We must speak up and make it okay to be present. Women have shut down, got derailed and confused in the past when confronting these issues. She was brow beaten into submission and feeling totally emotionally unsupported by her spouse, she walked out the door seeking separation, or worse, divorce! Sound familiar? I'm sure it does to some. Over 50% of all relationships end in separation or divorce. Not being heard, seen as neurotic or hormonal if she; disagreed, allowed herself to have an outburst, and her opinion not being taken seriously is a huge issue for women worldwide. In the community of women it is known and discussed, often! Women are often having to lie about being married, telling their mechanic or trades people that their husband will be upsct if this isn't done correctly. We have to navigate a world where men respect men, and not the independence or opinions of women.

Stronger women chose to go in competition with men, running their own business, working as hard, wearing black suits to fit in, climbing the corporate ladder, taking on male roles to prove their worth. Burning our bras, or joining them it seems, has not been the total answer to equality, even though it has added to our self esteem and given us value, and proven we are quite capable.

How can we have change and create new ways if we are not prepared to become the change?

It must begin in our speech, in our ability to recognise our 'sensitive truths' and to speak it to those that matter. We must go beyond fear, summon up the courage from a heartfelt place, to see it and speak it out loud, despite the historical biases and imbalances. When unspoken sensitive truths remain, we all become stuck, rendered stagnant, unable to move forward as whole beings. We must all intend to relate, communicate and create better community awareness if we wish to have balance restored. First we have to stop arguing, going round in circles from blame to victim-perpetrator, shame and anger, which the Patriarchal worldview bias currently feeds off.

We must embrace the healing offered to us via honouring the sacred feminine through embracing the Goddess, by re-embodying her and placing her back on the alter of wisdom where she belongs. The restoration of the sacred Feminine brings the way to wholeness for all humanity with her. First the Goddess must be acknowledged, remembered, revered and respected, honoured and put in the spotlight for a while, long enough to help create balance.

We need both the God and the Goddess, the divine masculine and the divine feminine equally, if we are to become whole.

Please don't be confused; this is not a religious thing we are talking about. This is an honouring of the core of each essence, male and female, yin and yang. Lets create new potential for wholeness within both sexes, healing the masculine and feminine schisms. Lets heal the damaged relationships and co-create the 'Sacred Union' in them once again. To do this we need to shift from a place of dominance and debate to a place of real dialogue and conversation.

We need to create a safe environment for that dialogue, which actually includes being heard, listening and expressing without blame. We need to create real empathy and caring with open hearts on both sides if we want to have a better understanding of each other. In our ancient cellular memory, we know that once upon a time the Masculine walked hand in hand and danced side by side with the Feminine and was not at war with her or trying to dominate or alienate her. There was once great love and harmony between the two.

Women need to embody the goddess to be empowered by her and feel the return of her divinity within, to transform the old karma and restore the sacred truths that will bring harmony and balance to both sexes. As the Goddess returns, bringing the sacred feminine, we become the midwives of the future, birthing a sacred 'Great Work' healing humanity back into wholeness.

Self Honouring Tips

1. Speak your truth lovingly from your heart and know it is always in service to others, no matter how uncomfortable.

2. Don't let anyone speak over you, or interrupt you ever again, tell them its disrespectful, arrogant and impolite.

3. Don't allow anyone to put you down or make you feel lesser than, instead make them accountable for their rudeness.

4. Listen to sexist comments and speak out about what you have just heard that is offensive to women-kind.

5. Embrace your sex; nurture and claim your inner woman, the intuitive, sensual and sensitive Goddess.

6. Hear your thoughts about the things that annoy you and approach the person they're about.

7. Work on self-improvement, become content with who you are rather than looking for approval from others.

8. Stop feeling pressured to be everything to everyone or to be something that you're not, you are perfect just as you are.

9. Take time out for yourself to regenerate from the pressures of everyday life, be kind, nurture and love yourself.

10. Practice patience, gentleness, kindness and forgiveness with yourself, remember that you too are a child of the universe.

11. Listen to your body and its natural rhythm, any pain, hurt or discomfort is telling you something about yourself.

Restoration of the Sacred Goddess

For too long now the sacred feminine has all but been ignored and suppressed. As a result, we have a world that's completely out of balance, a world that has run amuck, that is driven by money, power, consumerism, sex and greed. A world that is now in real crisis.

When the movie *"The DeVinci Code"* was unleashed into the world, it sent out a second call to all those connected to re-awaken and begin to heal the fractured sacred feminine. I felt this call, a call upon the Rose-line and the line of the sacred feminine of which many of us must play our part. This secret code, which acted as a key for many living Gods & Goddesses, was calling upon them to step up and to claim once again their sacred feminine heritage, to be put in their rightful place of power once again, which for eons had been hidden from the masses. That's right, it's not just women who need to claim the balance of the sacred feminine within them, men also have need of her balance.

Women all over the globe walked forward on mass and left behind all that was fake in their respective lives, all that was continually dishonouring them, all that was out of balance and not respectful to them anymore. It sent a cry from the Soul of the Goddess into the sacred wounds of long ago, for they needed to be healed and brought back into wholeness. And so this sacred pilgrimage was taken to task and the journey began on mass.

We all come from the Goddess

The Goddess needs to be brought back into play to take her rightful place in the bigger scheme of balance throughout our world. For with out her we are all bereft, left un-nourished, unfed, un-cared for and un-loved. You see it is the nurturing and life giving essence that births us all into being. Every living thing must come through and be graced and blessed by the Goddess. The God alone cannot give birth to anything, he must procreate through the goddess who acts as a sacred vessel for us all. The Goddess is a cosmic force that we feel mostly through our connection to Mother Earth, as she too is a cosmic being, part of a huge Solar system. The Goddess is therefore governed by certain universal laws and forces of nature, which mankind has studied and tried to exemplify in many synthetic ways.

She is the creative force of the universe that lives and breathes through us all, including our amazing planet Earth (Gaia) as Mother Nature. This truth has to take its rightful place once again in all that we do to be honoured and accepted as a universal truth. To not acknowledge this is to live a blatant lie, and dishonour her role in our lives. The Goddess does not take sides; she simply keeps the balance and is all-inclusive and nondiscriminatory. The forces of the elements and of life and death and rebirth are her domains. Mess with this and you have anarchy spinning out within natural cosmic forces. Mankind has embarrassed itself with its foolish ego fuelled belief it could actually cheat physical death. Something it gets a rude awakening from on a regular basis.

Duality and the fight for survival.

The Universe operates within a divine law of opposites that we call duality. This means that for every action there is an opposite reaction, and for every cause there is an effect. For example light becomes dark when the sunlight gives way to the moonlight at the end of each day as night approaches. The Yin Feminine energy has to interact with the Yang Masculine energies, attracting each other naturally as a consequence of existence and the need for procreation of most living species. This is the way it is and has been since before time, in fact the whole manifested universe seems to operate on this basic principal. Scientists demonstrate this best with the magnetic pull of opposites. Negative forces don't attract other negative forces they attract positive forces and vice versa. We all learnt this in primary school,
as it's basic science taught to most children who go to school.

Taking a closer look at nature and you can see what happens when something is dying out. When a fruit tree is threatened by extinction it throws out more seeds in fruits so that it can procreate, it sends a message to its feminine energy to make more fruit incase it dies. Nature knows that without this process it cannot sustain itself. It is built into the DNA structure of all living things for their survival. This is why farmers who grow certain fruit trees have
to prune each tree right back after harvest, so that new fruits will appear next season in abundance. They trick the tree into believing it is going to die or at least that it is under threat and so it throws out more seeds in its fruit. Just as nature calls upon this process to survive, so too is mankind.

It's the balance that the feminine brings that will sustain us once again.

We need the balance of the feminine to come in and save us all from the raping and pillaging of the very planet we live on. We are destroying her at such a fast rate, throwing Mother Nature more and more out of kilter; to such a point that scientists are saying that within 10 years we will be going into unknown survival territory, never yet experienced here on earth. Our atmosphere is already changing and this is affecting all life on the planet, especially our food sources, all agricultural farming, vegetation, crops, trees and animals alike.
It will affect our weather and change its climatic patterns, effecting rainfall frequency and temperatures. I remember being warned about this when I was in Primary school. Now it is on our doorstep and we have to do something about it and fast.

Many will say that this is all part of the big scheme as we have had many ages take place already upon Earth that man was not involved in, such as the
ice age and the dinosaurs' etc. While yes that is true to a point, but let us also realize that we have never had this kind of destruction from any living species including mankind to this degree affecting the planet before either. We are destroying the very heaven upon earth that exists for us already and that sustains our very living essence. We have become so reliant on technologies for
warmth and lighting, we do not remember how to live without them. Imagine not having electricity... what would we do? So much of our daily life is run by this one thing.

Restoring her true balance

The other reality is that Mother Earth will survive no matter what we do to her. She came from gas, molt and lava and so can return to gas, molt and lava. But the consequence is she will be uninhabitable, unable to sustain life as we know it. She does not need us to survive… but we as a living people, definitely need her to survive as a species. We feed of her, off her crops, fruits, and vegetables, off the waters from her lakes and rivers and we breather her fresh air through the trees abilities to create the oxygen we desperately all need. Gold, silver, gems and money will mean nothing if we have no water or food to eat. It is because of this silly arrogance that many are not taking any notice of her. Indigenous cultures around the world are more in awareness of this growing fact, for they are intrinsically connected to the earth. People are flocking to the cities believing that their salvation lies in numbers, only exacerbating an already huge over population problem. Farmers are slowly leaving the land they have worked for generations, as they cannot make ends meet in the financial climate.

By bringing the sacred feminine into play with mankind we will see a rise in concerns as women are connected to the earth much more than men.

As mothers we feel more strongly about human nature and the survival of our species is paramount to us. Women are more concerned with feeding their family than going off to fight religious based wars. Nuclear weapons are not going to help the survival of our species if the planet cannot sustain us anymore; we want good food and better health for our families and peace on earth. Trust me, it is not mothers who wish to send their babies off to war, especially when they have spent their entire lives feeding and nurturing them
into grown ups. We want to be considered and consulted in all decisions made for our communities, as 50% are women. For too long mostly men have been making the majority of the decisions that affected the masses. The tribes of our world's women weren't consulted and so everything has come out of old patriarchal male ideals and desires. This is not the balanced approach that the feminine would have demanded of them had they been consulted. Bereft of the feminine we are at war all the time on some level at some place in our world.

When you have men making all the decisions in the global family you have a family out of balance. Men are not usually the careers or nurtures; it is a feminine role, even if it comes from within a male. We all have both energies within us. For too long we have been catering to the dominant masculine side and not the feminine sides of our nature. It is time to come full circle and for us all to be brought back into balance before it is too late. Masculine and feminine must unite through wholeness and coexist in total respect and honour of each other's roles for survival if the world to have true balance restored.

Ode to the Goddess

How much of your life is spent trying to be perfect?

Trying to live up to all the expectations of what being a model woman, mother, lover, work colleague, friend and wife is perceived to be, can be exhausting to say the least. The demands that are placed on us are ridiculous.

For instance; we are supposed to look picture perfect even after mad, passionate sex - having performed in peak physical, emotional and spiritual balance with the Karma Sutra and Tantric techniques and experienced multiple orgasms. That's after you've casually whipped up a three-course gourmet meal for the lover/husband and 2.5 kids, finished a deadline for work so as to climb the corporate ladder for a promotion, taken little Jonnie to the dentist, the dog to the vet, picked up the dry cleaning, packed for hubby's business trip, bargain shopped for the week, balanced the cheque book and paid the bills, visited a sick friend and kept up all correspondence with the rellies. Having also given freely your spare time for a charity, read at least one best selling book, practiced yoga and completed your water aerobics routine, made time for a facial and new hair style, had your hands and feet manicured, finished studying your latest course, tackled all the house work, meditated for an hour and found the answer to world peace - all this and its only Monday!

Is it any wonder that women are having nervous breakdowns, visiting therapists trying to fathom how to live a more balanced life? Instead, why not just agree right now, that you are fed up with trying to be this perfect, and instead, accept that you already are PERFECTION! Every time you feel under pressure to be more than you are, read this desideratum of Self Acceptance. In fact put it where you'll see it every day to remind you of how futile it is to try to be more!

Self Acceptance Desiderata

I am a Goddess
I am an amazing Goddess.
I am all that I am, as a Goddess.
I accept the occasional bad hair day.
I accept that I am perfect just as I am.
I accept that I usually cry at soppy movies.
I accept that I like chocolate when feeling blue.
I allow myself to have time out and personal space.
I accept life's ups and downs with grace and humour.
I know that occasionally the bitch in me rears her head.
I accept my divinity in what ever form feels right for me.
I accept that I can have Baked Beans on toast and love it.
I accept that not everybody will understand me constantly.
I accept and allow all the perceived imperfections of others.
I accept that I do not have to be perfect in the eyes of others.
I accept that I am a Spirit having a very human experience.
I accept that I react to certain negative behavior from others.
I accept that there are some things that I am just not good at.
I accept that I do not have to be there for others all of the time.
I accept that I do not have to meet everyone's expectations of me.
I accept my friends and family, and love them just the way they are.
I accept that every day I am able to be new, different and spontaneous.
I accept that I can and often do change moods during the course of the day.
I accept that I am responsible for all of my reactions and emotional outbursts.
I accept that most days I am a genuinely kind and good person, at least I try to be.
I accept that my perceived physical imperfections are just illusions, I am truly beautiful.
I am realy an amazing
GODDESS!

Indulging the Goddess

As women the world over are learning to embrace their inner Goddess, wanting desperately to claim back their once lost feminine power more and more, they become aware that they need to feed and nurture this part of their spirit. The inner drive to explore one's infiniteness means indulging yourself by living fully, juicing up your life, celebrating your passions and connecting and playing with like-minded others. Seeking true balance means being open, willingly delving deep into the unknown, into the yet-to-be explored caverns of life, where the secret vistas of hidden mystery are waiting places within yourself wanting to become known by you. For too long women have hung back, felt compelled to fit in, to do what's considered right and expected of them all the time, as dutiful if not subservient women. It's time to break free and indulge your senses in who you are, on all levels.

To feel alive and connected to the wisdom of the Goddess is to be with her in totality, living passionately with purpose, unafraid of where she might take you within your self.

Indulge yourself, live beyond your wildest dreams; embark on the Goddess journey of a lifetime!

The inner Goddess is silently reverent, secretly watching over you but all the while present in your deeper lunar nature. She resides in your ability to embrace and enjoy your beauty and sensuality; she lives in your truth and in your need to feel confident by being real and authentic. She lives in your instinctual knowing and intuition and in your depth of feelings, in your moods and emotions and especially in your heart. Her inner frustration and pain dwells in your fears and anxieties, in your vulnerability and despair. She relates through your sexuality as lust and desire in your sensual nature and in your soul's need to feel lovingly connected to others. She also lives in your self-perceptions, in your heart's ability to let go and love deeply and unashamedly. She smiles in your compassion and kindness and weeps in your moments of raw emotion and inner turmoil.

So what part of your inner Goddess do you want or need to indulge?

To indulge means literally to give in to, to humour, to pamper, to spoil, to cater to, to gratify or satisfy… Sounds good to me, and I'm making a list right now, are you? The thing one indulges in doesn't have to be large, small spoils are fun, easy and just as enjoyable. Try starting small at first and work up to the larger indulgences. If you really want to give it some serious attention, then write out a comprehensive list. Begin with your Body and what it

needs, move onto the Mind, where do you want to mentally travel? Then onto your Emotions, what emotions would you most like to truly experience, and finally your Spirit, how can you set it free to be all it can be? What do these parts really want or need to experience? When was the last time you indulged yourself in a delicious way? There must be something you want to cater to, spoil or pamper yourself with…

> *"Becoming indulgent means allowing yourself to let go and have pure fun, spoiling yourself in the moment."*

Go on, indulge yourself, set yourself free in the moment:

Buy yourself a bunch of flowers.

Change your hair colour or style.

Take up a new hobby.

Do a relaxing exercise class.

Make yourself a mask.

Lie on the grass on the earth.

Invite a special friend for dinner.

Throw a girly pyjama party.

Have a massage or healing session.

Sleep in till late then get up and stay in your PJ's all day watching movies.

Read a new fantasy book.

Learn to play a musical instrument.

Join a group that does something you'd like to do i.e. hiking, scrap booking.

Take up painting or singing.

Make yourself a piece of clothing.

Buy yourself a divination tool like Tarot for fun.

Start your own sacred journal.

Have a hot bath with candles.

Write a letter to yourself.

Plan a special holiday to a magical place.

Try out a self-development workshop.

Create a sacred stone circle in your garden.

Plant some flowers in your back yard or balcony pots.

Dress up as a wild woman and go out with girlfriends.

Make a reason to celebrate.

Go for a long walk somewhere new.

Play with make up, finding new looks for hours of fun.

Buy a new outfit that's saucy.

Begin a fun morning ritual.

As a therapist I was always surprised just how many women put everyone else first, rarely, if ever, thinking about their needs or wants, let alone what they truly desired. Many I found had no idea what they would do if they could. They felt guilty doing something that was just for them. They didn't feel deserving and hadn't learnt how to give to themselves. It seemed to me to be a theme that women had adopted, like an urban myth that had slowly crept into the society of women the world over… Well I'm here to give the Goddess in you all total permission if you need it, to go out and learn to indulge in pleasure, pamper your every heart's wish with love and self gratification… learn to be a little selfish… hell won't freeze over! The Goddess responds to love, to kindness and caring, she loves to be playful and desires toys and fun. She wants you to experience anything your heart desires… So… What would do it for you right now? How do you want to feel? Go on indulge yourself with some small pleasure… I dare you.0

Indulging the Darker side!

The Goddess has many facets and allows us to explore all parts of our humanness both light and dark. She lives in the world of the great un-seen, veiled by denial, for fear of being made wrong, being judged or ostrisized. She unconditionally lets us feel all the otherwise lesser more undesirable human qualities and therefore helps us to explore our darker side, the naughty and sometimes wicked aspects of our Goddess nature. Judge if you like, but all our manipulation of others, laziness and apathy, envy and jealousy, anger and rage, self loathing and pity, our bad-girl behaviour and attitudes, all fall prey to her bringing us fully into balance. For how can we become whole if we cannot understand both extremities of our inner nature and its parameters?

How can we find our true balance within if we are not brave enough to face our ugly truths? How can we honestly set boundaries with authenticity and full integrity if we are not whole, still judging some part of ourselves as being wrong? It's just not possible to gain perspective without connecting with all parts of ourselves.

True power comes from a place of understanding and knowing oneself, a place of real confidence, a place of self acceptance, a place of tried and tested morals, a place of authentic working boundaries. This is a place of strength, a place of power of the no bullshit kind. It doesn't make you a bad person or Goddess, or wrong to have these otherwise less than desirable traits or feelings or the need to cater to them, it's just that we can all fall prey to our base human nature every now and then. To deny this is a lie, we can overcome them and check them if they get out of control, but first we must have dominion over them to do that.

I had a 43-year-old girlfriend say to me recently "I was such a goody-two-shoes, raised in an all girls Catholic boarding school and too afraid to give in to anything that might be considered as bad or wrong!" Bad for her meant anything where her parents or husband weren't in full control. She'd never allowed herself to cut loose; been to nightclubs and danced till dawn for instance, she'd never made love on a beach, or in a car. In fact she'd never left her hometown until recently, when her husband left her for a younger, wilder woman! After 25 years of marriage and being 'good' she now felt it was time to explore those dormant parts of her more hidden wilder self. She'd never indulged any part of herself. Well suffice to say she made up for lost time, as the pendulum swings from good to bad then finds its middle ground, so too did my girlfriend. She indulged in a midlife crisis that, while others may have judged it as being silly or ridiculous, was just an inner need, an itch that needed to be scratched, a dormant self that needed to take flight so as to find out who she was now, and it served her to do so. Right or wrong, good or bad, sometimes we just need to indulge ourselves and go there. Having given herself permission to move on and break through all those self imposed shackles that bound her; I can happily say that this girlfriend is a wiser, more open woman now.

What do you most need to give yourself at the moment?

Have you ever felt flat, out of sorts and not sure why? Have you looked in the mirror dissatisfied with yourself, unable to embrace your looks, your body or sensuality? Have you felt stuck in a rut, unsure how to get off that merry-go-round? Then it's time to seriously break free and become a little self-indulgent. If you have felt any of these things, no matter where you are in life at this time, stop, and tell yourself that you are an important person, that you do indeed love and appreciate yourself!

> *"Do I love myself enough to give myself all I need to be happy, to be authentically me, to be all that I could be?"*

Am I brave enough to explore myself and test my self-esteem and my arbitrarily set boundaries? What would it take for me to feel more alive and genuinely excited about my life? What part of myself have I forgotten to explore or feel I've left behind? Which part of me is out of balance and needs some attention? Now, where do you want to start? Simply make a decision right now to begin, and allow yourself out on the chain a little - no need to go crazy and do it all at once, there is plenty of time for more indulgence. But there is a need to learn to be true to your desires and to feel free enough to allow yourself to experience them at your leisure. All practicing Goddesses love to experience a little luxury and opulence, to feel appreciated and beautiful in whatever form is right for them, it honours their divine womanly essence!

Here are some indulgent self-nurturing ideas to stimulate you:

1 Notice the Magic in your life, those OMG how awesome, and Ooh la la moments. They stay in your memeory forever!

2 Dare to find and explore your inner passions, surrender and do what it is you most want to do.

3 Let the Wild woman out of the closet, let go and do something brave, bold and different.

4 Accept your beauty for the gift it is, explore and fall in love with your own awesome individuality.

5 Relax, and learn to revive your spirit, take time out to re-balance your equilibrium.

6 Learn to Laugh, Dance and Play often - become a happiness junkie or joybubble nazi…champagne helps with letting go! Its the bubbles!

7 Heal the past, forgive, release, then move on, otherwise the past cripples you in the now. If you cant, don't get angry … get even! Go create a better life and that will show em!

8 Live your dreams and find your joy, then life will be full of magic passion and wonder. No one will thanks you if you don't.

9. Spoil yourself with girly gifts and pleasures; go on indulge your wardrobe, buy some new bling and indulge with some wonderful perfumes or amazing oils.

10. Throw a party just because you want to, true eccentrics hold regular soirées, take a new Lovers, having ilicit affairs, exploring and indulging their sexual appetites.

11. Go places you've never been before, make time to explore some of our world's wonders. See exotic new locations just for the thrill of it.

The things that make the Goddess happier are lofty!

Part Two
Empowering the Goddess

What the Goddess Wants!

What I found was women were becoming more bereft of their inner connection to themselves, unable to understand their obvious complex feminine sensitivities.

However when asked, they more often than not knew exactly what they wanted from life in general terms. I watched women struggle to find a balance with their quality of life and their relations with others, while trying to work at their career and motherhood, while helping their family and friends feel loved. I was to observe that women had great courage and an amazing resilience to life. They are able to cope with huge things emotionally with amazing grace, especially when life seems to be falling apart. They were always ready to lend a hand to others and commit some of the most selfless acts of mankind. They worked hardest at avoiding conflict, always choosing the smoothest road through the difficult times. However, this wasn't always in their best interest. Women are deep complex and mysterious creatures with layered personalities and turbulent inner emotional tides that even Neptune would find hard to surf. They are governed by strong forces of nature that if they learn to ride, like a wild beast, makes them a force to be reckoned with.

Below are some insightful, if not helpful hints that if heeded would go a long way to healing some latent outmoded patterns in our society's social behavior towards our amazing fairer sex. Enjoy these very interesting findings! Overall I found that women placed a lot of importance on life values like respect, kindness, thoughtfulness and compassion, truth and sincerity, being honoured hallmarks of congenial conduct. I also found that women have quite lofty goals. They set very high standards and expectations, especially of themselves. Listening to these I realized how pressured women felt that they had to be perfect in pretty much all areas of their life. But as a result, in the workforce they were very capable to perform above and beyond their peer's expectations, often climbing the corporate ladder easily. I also discovered many women don't recognise their inner values and struggle to communicate them to those that matter. As a result of this, unspoken values can bring their life undone. Whenever someone inadvertently violates one of these unspoken inner values, women would shut down, withdraw and even shun or shut out that person. Feeling conflicted and unable to understand that it's okay to have these values, women need to learn that to speak them would set in place some healthy life boundaries.

In over 70% of the women I saw, they rarely if ever, felt beautiful and never felt powerful and always believed they were overweight whether they were or not. Their biggest complaints were usually; the treatment or misunderstandings they experienced with their partners; their struggles to manage the household budget and finances; too many demands made on their time; and - my personal favorite – "there's just not enough time for myself!"

What makes them Happiest?

Women ranked Pets, Sex, then Food– in that order, as the things that make them the happiest! Go figure! Women prefer and enjoy their animals more than their men! Pets it seems are more loyal and attentive: give constant approval and affection; adoringly loving looks; almost never complain; always love your appearance; dance when you enter a room; will go anywhere with you; love to share food; watch any TV program you like; are never judgemental; cheer you out of any bad mood and are happy all of the time. As a result of their pleasant and joyful countenance, any animal gaseous omissions are always forgiven and dismissed as normal behavior. Unlike their respective male homosapien counterparts, who should always remove themselves should such an occasion arise, especially socially.

Women love to be seen as:
Social

Socially, women are the heart of society and the creators of real community. Women frequently measure themselves by their relationships and the friends that surround them, always making time to catch up for coffee or lunch. They revel in social occasion and the joy it brings them, often going to great lengths to make it as pleasant a time as possible, attending to the minutest of details, all in honour of their guests. They take pride in their social status in a way that men rarely understand or do. It never goes unnoticed as they genuinely compliment each other about the effort that each has gone to for the occasion. Always socially supportive of those less fortunate, most women at some time in their lives find themselves helping out or involved with some kind of charitable organisation.

The qualities women most value in others

Sincerity

Women like the more refined, delicate qualities and value sincerity as number one. While she may never let on, a woman can always instinctively tell when someone is not being genuine and sincere. When someone is being sincere, an inner sensitivity and true connection are being made with that person. Sincerity demonstrates inner qualities such as honesty and truthfulness, respectfulness, and real interest. These are all amiable and affable qualities. Being sincere shows a depth of thoughtfulness and displays a genuine desire to be authentic when communicating and dealing with others.

Sensitivity

Women like people who actively demonstrate some sensitivity towards their delicate feminine nature. Genuine sensitivity implies emotional intelligence and empathy, coupled with awareness and compassion for a situation and those involved. Sensitivity fosters respect and trust within women and breeds a sense of emotional openness and safety when feeling vulnerable, fragile or exposed. Women respect people who are sensitive and emotionally mindful, aware of the impact life has on their feelings. Being sensitive and emotional creatures, women feel everything and therefore need their feelings to be understood! Aggressive, crass or vulgar communication or behaviour shuts their inner sensitivity down faster than the speed of light.

Acceptance

One of the most appealing qualities for women today is acceptance. All women want to be accepted for who they are. Acceptance shows an openness and allowance of all parts of her to be on display without fear of ridicule or judgement. A truly sophisticated quality, acceptance is a major key in her feeling safe to display her inner feelings to others. Inner and outer acceptance allows a sense of personal freedom and is vital for her being able to explore more of her own potential. With all the pressures placed on women in society today, acceptance of her total nature will go a long way to healing her past suppressions.

What women want more of

Time

Ranking number one, it seems women want more time in their lives. As women entered the work force in droves and were also left to raise the children, time became very important to them. When asked what they wanted more of, time ranked above love! I found that incredible, but I understood as the demands that are placed on the average women have increased. What she has to fit into her life on daily basis is absurd. Time it seems, is the greater need to help keep life flowing, to 'make it all happen', to balance conflicting priorities; love, work, friends, and home life, making the right but tough decisions.

Money

As the financial demands of today's living increases and the social pressures grow, so too does the need for more money. Women ranked money more important than love but not more important than time. Not for it's own sake, but for better control of spending and saving wisely. Women's need to help provide and to become successful has developed their relationship to earning more money, as well as affecting and stimulating their social self-esteem. The rise of many home based businesses is attributed to having enabled and encouraged women in particular to become independent and successful while still raising and looking after their families. Did you know that approximately 46% of women who own their own business run it from home? That's a 20% increase in the last five years.

Love

Women want more lasting, long-term, loving relationships. Love is a key factor to a woman's inner and outer balance. She feels whole when in love. Giving and receiving love and being in a union with a significant other fulfills her innate need to be caring and nurturing. Feeling loved is part of her connectedness to herself. When she loves her partner, she feels content. While being loved is a primal desire within all mankind, for women it is a natural part of their intrinsic feminine nature. To a woman, love represents being appreciated, respected, honoured, and cared for and is an important part of her social status. A woman will go out of her way, even suffer in service to those she loves;

Fulfilment

Women want the freedom to pursue what ever gives them purpose and makes them feel satisfied with life. Personal fulfilment has been an illusive part of life in the past, often overshadowed by the needs of her family and loved one's demands on her time. While loving them is an important part of her, there are other things she wants to experience and find out about. Experimenting with the creative person within is necessary if she is to find out what stimulates and fulfils her creative side. Making time to find her passions is important to her evolvement and ultimate feelings of satisfaction and fulfilment.

What women want most from men!

Respect

Women everywhere are over misogynistic narcissism from men in general terms. So respect is now part of the natural order for women today. Arrogance is no longer tolerated, nor is bullying and intimidating tactics. Nothing shuts women down faster! Tolerance and acceptance are all needed as part of respecting another human being's right to be themselves. Aretha got it right - women want R.E.S.P.E.C.T! It encompasses many things for them; personal privacy, their physical space and belongings; different viewpoints, philosophies, religion, gender, lifestyle, ethnic origin, physical ability, beliefs, ideas, knowledge, and personality. There is mental respect, emotional respect, physical respect and spiritual respect - she wants it all!

Romantic Dates

Besides love, women wanted their partners and significant others to date them more often. Romance is the glue that keeps a love relationship alive and passionate. When romance is forgotten, the love can wain and struggle to stay alive. It seems dating is the one thing men need to do a lot more of. Women deserve to feel special, honoured, wooed and spoilt. Just a little! It's not about how expensive it is it's about the thoughtfulness that goes into thinking about and organizing it. That her man takes her on romantic date means a lot to her; it says 'I love you' in a very special way. Remembering significant romantic events and dates are important to women and help to maintain the romance in their relationship. However men quite often need prompting and coercing in this department sadly… When sex is most likely to be the outcome of such an auspicious time, one questions and seeks an answer as to why this seems so hard?

To be listened to

It was one of the things women complained the most about to me. They wanted to be heard, listened to and most importantly, understood. Nothing feels less validating for a woman than when someone you are talking to butts into the conversation and starts to talk about something else - or worse – talking about themselves. It's considered the height of rudeness by women the world over. Men are the worst at this. Women just need to be heard. So listening to them is important. Simple. What's interesting is they don't mind if you don't always get what they are saying, but its definitely important for her to feel that you care enough to take time and just listen. Listening doesn't mean fixing anything, it just means listening. This one thing could actually save a lot of relationships.

Help with Chores

Women want their partners to help out around the house more with the everyday simple chores. Women want their men to be thoughtful and help out around the house without being nagged. She doesn't want to have to constantly ask her man for help. Rather she wants him to recognise what needs doing regularly and offer to do little things to help her. If he can set up the garage, stereo and television and remember how to care for the car and the garden regularly, then he can also fill a dishwasher or washing machine, or hang out or fold up clothes and put dishes away occasionally. It's these little things that please her and frustrate her.

What women wanted from sex:

Orgasms

Yes you guessed it - women want more orgasms! It seems since the revolutionary openness of 60's free love, women now feel okay about and want more of the big O. Orgasm is a fabulous all over stress relief. As women are experiencing more pressure in their lives, more orgasms is a good coping mechanism…Yay! The fact that it's free, un-taxable, gives off heaps of endorphins and an amazingly youthful glow, is a great body workout and helps our cardiovascular system might have something to do with it. I found women just love to have sex! Even though it gets messy and can be incredibly awkward and often undignified, women are more comfortable about it and just love it. It seems with the growth of women working and staying single longer, their sexual exploitations have become more interesting and they love to share. The desire to be wild and experimental, taking a little more control in the bedroom equates to wanting more pleasure and orgasms. Well hallelujah to that I say!

Foreplay

Even though like men, women want an orgasm and it's the desired end result of sex, women still want more foreplay. Foreplay is important as it sets the centre stage for great sex as compared to just a quick romp. There are seven levels of arousal for women and as a result of each level being stimulated; there are seven levels of juice her vagina creates. I bet many of you didn't know that. Each level allows her to become juicier and therefore the pleasure factor for her increases 10 fold. That's got to be good for both parties don't you think? Taking time to sex up first is big on the list for great sex for women. Find new ways to be aroused and get playful with foreplay. There are some great sex toys now specifically designed for women's pleasure, so don't be afraid to communicate what you need or want and be playful with foreplay.

Emotional connection

While we all want the mechanics of sex to be working and there is the geography of the body to navigate, it's the emotional component for many women that's often missing. Feeling connected to her sexual partner is very important to her inner needs in order to feel completely engaged on all levels. Women need to feel their partners on many levels, so sharing feelings about each other and opening up emotionally help her to relax and connect. It's the heart part that allows her to feel cherished and loved. Yes, women still want to feel loved by their sexual partner, especially long-term partners. One-night stands are usually lust-based romps and are rarely a great emotional connection. Sadly, many women try to turn a weekend of lust into a lifetime of love and fail. Real relating and great sex come from developing a good emotional connection with your partner.

Goddess in the Boardroom

The emerging Goddess culture in the boardroom is seeing a new breed of woman. These women have cleverly refined and unified aspects of their masculine (mental) and feminine (feeling) qualities into their brand of business acumen. Consequently these emerging executive Goddesses are considered to be having a profound long term healing effect in the business sector and corporate realms.

Her presence at the very highest levels of management seems to be necessitating and even driving 4th dimensional awareness and concepts back into our 3rd dimensional world of commercial business. This has a flow on effect transforming everything from outmoded humanities and older managerial models and techniques, to helping create a balance within humane, ethically developed business strategies along with fair-trading, while birthing a healthier, holistically improved corporate citizen. Not bad given that women only make up approximately 10% of the corporate sector. Imagine how balanced business life would be if it were even at 30%!

Hallelujah… all hail the Corporate Goddesses in the boardroom!

Over the past five decades women have come a long way. Where female managers were once invisible and largely nonexistent, there has been steady movement up and out of administration roles and into the realms of management and high-powered positions within the corporate world, including national and global politics. However, sometimes this was at the expense of her personal suffering, judgement and ridicule, the need to even martyr herself to some degree, and having to succumb to the competition with men. In the past women have had a hard time wrestling with this balance, especially the outward social judgements of their role in working society, of course this has changed. She is now accepted as a professional and no longer needs to overcome these old social biases, or has she?

I remember a time in my early 20's when a female client ridiculed me for working, because I had to place my children in day-care full time. She was simply projecting her social beliefs of what she saw as a 'women's role' in society back then. My life circumstances didn't allow me the privilege of being a stay at home mum. Well 25 years on, things have changed dramatically; I, like many of my peers, am now the CEO of my own company and totally love what I do, my children are grown and I'm getting on with the fun of business.

As a therapist having held counsel with many business women, I observed a shared commonality of certain traits, motivations, behaviours and life experiences that set them apart and predisposed them as non-conformists in their life's direction and choices. Often they were the eldest daughters who'd had huge responsibility placed on them early. Some were consciously choosing not to marry or become mothers early in their life. They were simply choosing a different lifestyle, one that was not considered by their mothers before them. These women want to succeed in their chosen vocation testing themselves in the world before settling down to become wives and mothers.

I observed first hand how feminine analytical wisdom could be adapted to the strategic requirements of business and utilised in many corporate situations, even politics. It definitely takes a certain kind of woman with specific developed qualities to feel comfortable enough to be completely at home in the realms of business and/or working with men. But when she can, she brings some interestingly developed feminine skills along with her. These Goddesses had to face the masculine within to be able to handle the masculine without. Sometimes that meant she'd been able to identify herself through a good relationship with her role model father. After all, she knows that she is a woman operating in a man's world if she's in business. She's had to develop her mental, logical, and rational masculine side for men to accept her as a comrade and an equal.

In the past however this often came at the cost of a Goddess rejecting her unconscious, vulnerable, emotional, feminine side, possibly even hiding her latent psychic and natural intuitive abilities, choosing instead to hone her mental agility and analytical power as her new, preferred, intellectual armour. These Goddesses have had to give way to an achievement-oriented persona, combining the qualities of the warrior with that of a cool, strategic, fast thinker, developing her intellectual linguistic approaches.

Goddesses in business today are learning to balance their intuitive feminine wisdom with their intellectual versatility giving them powerful observational abilities. She is therefore a force to reckon with. This kind of mastery consequently opens the dark, primitive, deeper side of her inner goddess nature, allowing her to see and penetrate both sides of an equation through emotional intelligence and mental objectivity; a great analytical requirement used in both strategic business planning, management, and of course, leadership.

These Goddesses are very powerful women indeed; very focussed, usually quite driven, with loftier goals in mind - qualities that I too had developed over a period of time. I recognised that my female business clients were mirroring many of my strengths even though they were used in different ways. These Goddesses were wise, intelligent, courageous women, having faced many life crises and developed mastery over their financial independence. They were often living alone feeling that to be independent meant not having a permanent live in partner. I observed that many were oftentimes divorced, seen as ruthless, and found it difficult to find partners they felt were intellectually equal to them. They all possessed that feminine wisdom of insight and had a penetrating perception, effectively used to see beneath the surface of things, to the root of a problem. These qualities gave them an intellectual psychological edge in their business, with the ability to bring the unconscious into conscious awareness. Maybe that's why some men found them formidable and couldn't be around them. When a woman can see all and is unafraid of making you accountable, there's nowhere to run. But one thing is for sure; all these corporate amazons were heart driven, fully present in their soul's passions, fearless of life and its challenges, fuelled by the desire to be great at whatever they choose to do.

Developing Corporate Soul

When we have real world, modern, archetypal Corporate Goddesses like the late Anita Roddick of the Body Shop empire, who bravely lead the way, set the pace, and work in conjunction with the ultimate truth that we can no longer ignore the corporate rape and pillaging of our planet's resources, then we have a changing sea of consciousness, a sea that needs a new breed of sailors willing to navigate its choppy corporate waters.

Goddesses in business today are learning to balance their intuitive feminine wisdom with their intellectual versatility giving them powerful observational agility. She is therefore a force to reckon with.

As a result of this new breed of archetypal Joan of Arcs, flexing their ethical, cultural muscles, seeking accountability for the past mistakes of the arrogant, greedy corporatist, the social conscience of big business has to step up. As Mother Earth's natural changing cycles have their way with us, so too corporate business must change and let go of the need to negate or control her for instant profiteering. We must flow with her in the organic cyclic dance of life, whilst looking after future generations with responsible Earth Care tactics. After all, the ultimate role of the Goddess is to look after her global children.

Women naturally look to serve all within their heartfelt community conscience; it's their desire to see integrated heart placed within all realms of society including business. The Goddess Cosmology is one of the unity of heart intelligence – which is seen as the secret of all measure. Spiritual ethical business is the desire to develop corporate soul for all those truly connected to the humanitarian global picture.

The ancient tribal Goddesses knew that it was their job to leave something to help regenerate and serve those generations yet to come. In this manner they honoured their earth walk story, their carbon footprints remained light and were easily supported by the energetic web of all life. They understood naturally and ethically that everything we did was indeed connected to everyone in existence.

So nothing on any level was ever even considered if it could be harmful to human existence in the long term. Whether lofty ideals or infinite wisdom, this rings of truth for ultimate business conduct for the future. Evidence of the ancient temples where the Goddess was worshiped and consulted on all matters of state, still live on in the dimmest recesses of our deeper subconscious memory bank for both men and women. However it has been all but buried and denied in our modern western society. Mythology and history have blended many a powerful female role model for modern women who seek the remembrance and knowledge of how women were once also great and capable leaders.

Setting Standards & Living the Reality to Create a Better Business Culture!

- Use strong symbolism to ground your cultural identity.
- Set your spiritual values and write your mission statement for all to see.
- Measure what you do long term with the effect it will have on everyone.
- Incorporate development and growth for employees / team affiliates.
- Have small empowering meetings to reinforce your principals and awareness.
- Lead by example: inspire others by setting the tone at a leadership level and others will follow.
- Love your work it then becomes a heart felt worship.
- Dream your story – let the journey be fun and meaningful while dreaming big.
- Share your passion - sparking purpose based on inner desire, but keep it real.
- Let magic happen by allowing the natural unfolding of your ideas, step by step.
- Be open to the synchronic events as the universe lines up with your intent and needs.
- Weed the path of old energies and attachments that no longer serve, let go of perceived outcomes as they may limit you.
- Accept that true mastery in business alchemy means constant refining of your path – you lose nothing through progression.
- Reset standards and conduct that aligns with where you choose to go – move forward in strength, in balance, in alignment with your truths.

Only work with those who align with your values – don't feel the need to sell out to those who do not share the same, or rescue others by trying to convince them of yours.

Lead by example; inspire others, by setting the tone at leadership level and others will naturally follow.

Developing true Goddess qualities...

During my global travels and times as a therapist, I observed certain qualities that set true Goddesses apart from ordinary women. These women are dynamic and have an air about them - a kind of soiré de vive (*lust for life*) energy, which oozes out of their every pore. And it's this enigmatic lust for life that enriches everyone who meets them. People are naturally drawn to them, like magnets they attract others who happily hang out in their energy, for the sheer delight and magical feeling that their presence offers. Encounters with them can often be healing and hypnotically transforming - leaving you feeling happy, uplifted, motivated and deeply inspired. They are positive and elevating, emanating an easygoing naturalness that on closer inspection possesses an undeniable confidence and inner emotional power.

I found these women to be genuinely caring and discerning, displaying qualities of natural leadership and quietly appearing as modern-day Queens of our society. They generously offered counsel to those around them who sought out their brand of wisdom, heartfelt honesty and genuine compassion. These amazing women stood out from the crowd as being special energetically and I couldn't help but notice them. I made it my business to surround myself with them - and many I now happily call friends. Why is this? What do these women posses that others don't?

What in essence makes a true Goddess?

Essentially, she is your unique embodiment of a potent, very feminine and inspiring woman. She is a natural leader because she carries a wise influential energy regardless of her age, social or financial status. She is contagiously in love with life, at peace with herself and genuinely connects with others. She naturally has the audacity to live her truth and be authentically herself. Speaking from her heart a true Goddess willingly shares her truth, knowledge and wisdom with love. She is unafraid to express her own creativeness with style and flair, and she delights in all of life's passions - finding beauty in almost everything. Most of all, a true Goddess has the courage and zest it takes to break through innate conditioning and go for what she loves.

A true Goddess embodies all that is beautiful and sensual, warm and inspiring, discerning and fair.

Before we go any further lets be very clear about what a Goddess is not: In the past 100 years we have seen the rise and developments of some very interesting feminine energy stereotypes. However, none of these depict the essence of a real Goddess or her true qualities. For instance, a true Goddess is not a dumbed down, agreeable and submissive chirpy bimbette, tied to the kitchen baking cookies and wearing pink. Feminine energy is not a saccharine almost austere Betty Crocker clone, nor is she the perfect plastic woman - depicted in Desperate House Wives either. She is not a sex-crazed dominatrix who uses her sex to control, bully or whip her men into shape and submission, and she is definitely not a bra-burning anti-men, hardened feminist, even if she happens to be gay. These feminine stereotypes have nothing to do with the true qualities embodied by a genuine Goddess. And let me be clear that goddessdom has nothing to do with sexual preference or lifestyle choices, true Goddesses are found in all walks of life.

Indeed the true Goddess is a nurturer - but she's no submissive slave.

Yes, she is open and receptive - but she's not a doormat either. She is gentle and soft and kind, but she is not a wallflower. And while yes, she can be very strong and tenacious, she doesn't need to be a ball-breaker or use aggressive behavior.

The True Goddess In Everyday Life

Thinking about your own source of strength is the first step to finding your true Goddess. Is it masculine or feminine? Does feeling powerful seem testing and awkward - or profound and effortless? Does being feminine feel uncomfortable and foreign to you? Who did you see as holding the power at home as a child?

Understanding the basic Goddess archetype energies and attributes helps us to align with those qualities as we observe their traits within our own character. We can then learn how best to relate these wise qualities by applying them in everyday life situations.

Here are some questions to get you thinking about your power and its strengths:

1. How do you get your way in the office? How do you get your way with men?

    Be really honest with yourself and notice your strategy unfold: For example, when do you push, demand, sulk, manipulate, calculate, flirt, get angry or scheme? Whenever you do any of these things you are using control dramas and not true Goddess feminine power.

2. Next, think about when you feel like a Goddess? Who are you around? What are you doing? What qualities do you embody in that space – open, loving, patient, playful, sensual, joyful or in flow? What ever encourages you to move into this space – do more of that.

3. Are you different at work to how you are with men? Why and what motivates you to act in these ways?

4. Who are your role models? And what have you patterned from these peers? What is actually a decision you have made independent of peer/social pressure?

5. What can you do different to remain in your Goddess energy for longer? What do you feel this would achieve for you?

6. And finally, what does being a Goddess mean to you? Who do you think is a true Goddess walking the earth, and why?

7. How much of what you do is based on your emotion or on the reality of the situation?

8. How often to you dodge your true feelings, afraid they may make you feel insecure?

9. What calls you to action - to respond in strength and to own a truth?

Why All This Is Especially Important Today!

Nature's survival requires perfect balance and harmony with everything co-existing. Summer balances winter, water balances fire, night balances day, yin and yang, masculine and feminine. It's not rocket science to realize Mother Nature has her own power – that is natural and not contrived.

However, if you look around at the concentration of world leaders, the philosophers who have influenced us, the way the schooling, educational and medical systems are organized and general positions of authority – it has all been overwhelmingly structured by male energy. It's only since the suffragettes sought the vote that women have started to have any say in the way things are done. But given that about only 10 per cent of the corporate world is women, you still have an unbalanced society rule when it comes to decisions that affect us all.

Now, I am not saying that men haven't been doing a good job - as there are some men who are conscious, self aware and mature - who bring forth many great qualities and initiate, bold, strategic, self-sacrificing changes in the name of loving service. But the truth is power and greed has fueled them the most and we can see the scars of it everywhere.

Male-energy when it goes uncurbed by a feminine counter-balance, begins to lose control. And we have been witnessing this in the world for some time. Left unchecked it becomes arrogant, defensive, stubborn and aggressive - initiating wars and the like. Trust me it's not mothers who send their boys off to war – it's men!

But the reality is - men are not entirely to blame. They are just responding unconsciously to a lack of authentic strong and empowered feminine energy. And in my experience, as a therapist, most women have little access to the concept of what that actually is. It was this very thing that inspired me 10 years ago to start my magazines and write my books.

The essence of Divine Feminine power has been suppressed for so long, that there are not enough women on the planet today who are really connected and aware of it to live it fully and teach others. We are all on the journey of reclaiming the sacred feminine, and I am merely inviting you to step into the void with me. There are definitely some women living this truth, but not enough to create any massive global turn-around at the moment. I believe it's western women who will instigate a greater change, as we are the ones who began this in the first place. We must be brave and committed to letting go of the old conditioning, so that our daughters and grand daughters can live in a more harmonious and balanced global society alongside their men folk.

Men and women are drawn to a Goddess, because being around her makes everyone feel enriched.

The Potency Of Feminine Energy

The reality is, true feminine energy is very potent and powerful - it could easily go head to head with male power. But that is not what we are wanting, there is no need for competition of who's greater and who is not, as both sexes have equal and different strengths. They were made different to cooperate and co-create in divine union together - joined in relationship with the heart through love. Women in their divine feminine bring out the best in men - just as we crave men who are strong, protective, fair yet decisive, self-assured and effortless leaders. It is wise to note that men are also crying out for women who are feminine, soft, gentle, sensual, stable and receptive co-creators. At no time is it necessary to emasculate men to be equal. Women need to cease thinking that men actually owe us something - as I realise that they don't. After all our men of today are not responsible for what took place hundreds of years ago, even if they carry the genetic memory in their male DNA.

As we help raise more sons and daughters we must make them aware of this important balance in respect of each other's gender as they grow up, and set a new standard through awareness in our offspring. This is our job as parents and mothers, to bring balance back into the new generations who will soon walk this earth as Gods and Goddesses.

I believe we owe it to ourselves, first and foremost to honour our return to our divine feminine essence, rediscovering for ourselves our true Goddess qualities - claiming their power and truths. This is our birthright, something we must gift back to ourselves.

Here are some true Goddess Qualities to embrace:

Sensual - accepting of ones voluptuousness and soft feminine curves being very naturally sexual by nature.

Powerful - she is respected as an influential and authoritative and reliable woman, able to take control and lead.

Intelligent - mentally clever, sensible and rational - able to process data, analyse and be self-regulating.

Beautiful - not afraid to accentuate and make the most of her natural beauty, with make up, colour and clothing.

Stylish - she is happy to look gorgeous and stunning using bejewelled adornments and elegant flattering clothing.

Receptive - able to receive love and new things openly and including different points of view, new ideas, and concepts.

Patient - able to be tolerant and persevering - choosing to remain uncomplaining while waiting for something.

Wise - able to share her shrewd knowing usually learnt first hand from experience with others as wisdom.

Compassionate – displaying kindness, she's openly sensitive and concerned for the welfare of others affected by life's awkward circumstances.

Authentic - she is original, genuinely real and true to herself, relating this to others makes her trustworthy and not false.

Strength - having proven her resilience to life she is a source of inner support and emotional powerhouse for others.

Grace - she has elegance, generosity of spirit, inner refined politeness and loveliness - virtues valued in one's afterlife.

Eloquence - she has noble speaking ability and chooses her words carefully, able to express and articulate with diplomacy, fluency and grace.

Loving - she has no issue being tender, warm or affectionate, or being doting or devoted to those she cares about and truly loves.

Truthful - always honest and known for her sincerity - being genuinely moral and respected as upright and trustworthy. Passionate - she is always enthusiastic, displaying intense emotional desire and drive for what she truly believes in.

Nurturing - she is able to encourage and take care of something or someone and see things flourish and grow.

Confidence - she displays a genuine self assurance and belief in her own abilities, skills and talents, and is driven to follow it through.

Discerning - she is able to analytically weigh things up, while being perceptive and discriminating and selective in her judgements.

Pathways to the Goddess

Empathy & Compassion

There are many ways we can learn to connect to another human being, but one of the first ways is through sympathetic alignment. Sympathy is usually expressed when we are in agreement with another mind, appearing to be in some kind of alignment or in compatibility with that other. It is easily spotted with in like-minded groups, whereby people show a sympathy to those who have shared similar experiences, backgrounds or upbringing, or who's travail's or crisis in life tend to match their own. They can also be sympathetic due to causes, beliefs, and ideals or shared ideas. Sympathy, while being a legitimate aspect of human intimacy, which helps us to connect, is really a product of the mind, and aligns with the third chakra, the Solar plexus.

Love however combines the first, second and third chakras creating a synthesis before arriving at the fourth chakra the heart centre, giving rise to the term 'heart consciousness'. This happens because through the second chakra we are able to take sympathy into our emotional state, which creates 'empathic sensing'. Here we use our emotional feelings so we can align to actually feel the same as the other person. True empathy is a gift that needs to be honed.

We do this by projecting ourselves mentally into the other person's reality, emotionally connecting to it, and bringing those emotions back into our own body. In that moment our feelings are converted to match their feelings. We take on their feeling reality in whatever state it's in. Of course some people develop this much easier than others. In case you were wondering, yes, it's a developed skill, that anyone can learn. With empathy we get to feel and perceive from their perspective, allowing us to see things from their experience and point of being.

There is a wise old saying…

"The heart sees what the mind cannot yet comprehend."

Which simply suggest that the heart (fourth chakra) has a better understanding of things, and aligns with a deeper set of emotional drives, accessing a deeper knowing as to why some things happen the way they do. In other words it has a timeless wisdom derived from true heart consciousness. The heart is the point of being, a divine portal and seat of the soul, which connects us to the divine feminine self. Therefore empathy is the first step to opening the heart chakra and begins the process of developing the art of real compassion.

The realisation of Compassion is brought into awareness through the fifth chakra. This is the throat chakra and aligns with the nervous system in the body and expresses itself through the voice box, which is the centre of manifestation and communication on the physical plane. Compassion like love is an action and functional energy – and gifts one with the ability to connect to others. Complete strangers can therefore demonstrate compassion, by showing sympathy (alignment & understanding) with feeling (caring) for someone, regardless of their racial or socio-economic or cultural background. These people have no 'reason' (agenda) to love or to bond with that person, but they do it anyway…

This is true compassion. It is kindness, caring and thoughtfulness and mindfulness all wrapped up in one moment of complete connection.

This demonstrates that they can give love without conditions; this is what is called true selfless (Buddhist, Christ and Goddess) compassion! If we have true compassion, we have the ability to encompass everything and anything within ourselves, we can absorb it, hold onto it without it consuming our energy. It is a fusing of the self with the other in a perfect state. It means the one who carries this has the ability to naturally emanate their love vibration to everyone and everything. The heart is the teacher, the healer and true spiritual pathway for humanity. By keeping the heart centre open practicing love, compassion and wisdom we can transcend anything, resolve all conflict and clear any darkness that stands between our heart and us.

Once that is done our heart and mind become united, open to universal heart values and ethical flow in compassionate love for our planet and all sentient beings in the universe. Adepts of the Goddess path, whether male or female, have mastered the process of creation: that being of fertilization, creation and gestation of life itself, giving birth to that life. No matter whether that life is a project, idea, business, situation or being that needs to be birthed into physical reality. They have learned to nourish, care for that life until it seeks its own destiny path. When we are heart centred, we allow that life to fulfil its own destiny with out need to control it. To do otherwise would be to smother love it, to try to control it might block it somehow. So in loving something we must learn to let it go, let it fly, let it be true to itself, to be truly in flow with its own divinity, to trust that in the divine process it will do what ever it came into being to do, no matter what the result. Ultimate trust is part of real compassion and has a unique level of understanding and acceptance of radical trust in all processes... even if it feels like a death of sorts to let go of something, this is what ultimate compassion demands we do, surrender to unconditional LOVE.

Develop Healthy Goddess Attitudes

A woman with attitude has a wise worldly voice and is unafraid of making decisions, or being true to herself, living her unique goals with self-respect and dignity.

Imagine every day waking up with the most powerful of thoughts and feelings about yourself and your life, embracing each day with amazing uplifting energy, happy with your world - is this possible you ask? Yes it definitely is.
To be the best goddess you can be means being a real woman and developing healthy positive attitudes to live by. There are many attributes that set people apart in general, but developing positive personal attitudes is the key to becoming true to yourself and living a much more authentic happy existence.

When something becomes an attitude, it becomes an integrated habit, a behaviour if you like, and a way of being. Our attitudes define our core values and becomes part of our innate character; they define our conduct and become part of our living integrity. Develop bad attitudes and every one will give you a wide birth as they avoid your negativity. Develop good and positive attitudes and watch as everyone who gets to know you wants to hang out with you as you give off confidence and good vibes. There is a saying that we catch fleas of dogs. What this means in essence is that when you hang out with someone you end up catching things off them - attitudes just being one of them.

Become a real goddess who celebrates herself often, In love with her body, and intelligent mind, Who knows and believes she's more than enough.

For far too long women were held back and suppressed in society, and while we have come a long way from legislating for the right to vote or to being accepted in the work force, we still have a long way to go. There can only be true equality when we develop self-respect and create healthy attitudes related to who we are as individuals. This attitude then needs to penetrate from within to without and be felt everywhere we are present. Many women are still totally dependant on men for their complete existence and therefore oftentimes have had by default to compromise themselves in some way. Many have been afraid to be creative and express themselves as strong whole individuals afraid of losing their mate. Still branded the weaker sex, women have been trying to prove their strengths by joining the men and playing at life from their rules. Well no more. Girl power is on the increase, not from a dominant male place, but from a quiet feminine innerness that reveres her true greatness with grace and power. Women want to take back their self respect and find their own path out of silent but ever present tyranny. No longer does being married or having family mean that you cannot run a business, be a creative and expressive individual, nor compromise your need to be loved if you truly want to.

Allow her inner spirit to be set free, see beyond the old horizons, Embracing life's challenges with humour and grace.

On the other hand many men have recognised this need within women and actually support their partner's growth. It's not our men's fault we are they way we are. We are different and are meant to be the mothers and nurturers and care givers of the planet. Men are naturally the warriors and hunter-gatherers and are meant to take care of and protect their family in their own ways. But nowhere was this meant to be oppressive to their women folk or undermine her role as life giver, nurturer and carer. I have met husbands who ask me "how can I help my wife develop self-esteem"? If women don't believe in their innate goodness and beauty then it's hard for their men who grow tired of having to constantly prop them up emotionally.

If you don't love or believe in yourself, no amount of compliments or positive words from others are going to make a difference to your self esteem, even if you crave their attentions. Many divorces have come about due to this and the fact that women have to learn to love themselves - before they can receive love fully from others. It all boils down to developing some positive healthy attitudes, letting go of the past out dated ones, and living the empowered self rebirthed. It's too easy to blame others for our lacking, or hurting - we must heal any wounds and reveal our souls to ourselves to be recognised for their own greatness. We can no longer rely on others to prop us up and so be prepared to shed the old skins as you generate a more positive outlook that supports you being all that you can be - a goddess with a new empowered attitude.

Script your own life's path and create magic for yourself and others, Sharing the beauty of your ever unfolding journey with rapture, Empowering others who need your loving wise counsel.

So how do we change old attitudes?

Develop an attitude of self love:
This acquaints to practicing loving thoughts, personal wellbeing and positive self care, by taking pride in ones self through self loving acts. There is a need for self-honouring your emotional goodness, your body, your intelligent mind with self respecting kindness, like taking time out. Loving yourself is learning to celebrate who you are. When we love our self we allow the grace to feel wholeness and so naturally recognise when we are under duress or out of balance and do

something about it. Allowing yourself to feel and become gently and gracefully proud of who you are. When we are loving and kind to our self others will also be. Learn to love your own quirkiness and individuality reflected in your personality. Become loving and kind and relax in the heart of true self-love.

Develop an attitude of respect:
This acquaints to accepting that everyone is different to you and that you do not need to know everything but should respect the rights of others as you would wish them to respect your rights also. Finding that balance between setting some healthy boundaries that create self respect is important, however, its also about allowance, tolerance and acceptance. The Buddhists call this mindfulness, and respectfulness is when you simply observe rather than participate in judgment. Everything has a right to be respected for who and what it is this includes you. If there is any part of yourself that you need to learn to respect, trust me you will attract people who somehow will bring this lesson to your attention. Respect honours everything as being in its rightful place in the big scheme of things. Self-respect honours you being true to you and it is very healthy indeed.

Develop an attitude of honesty:
This acquaints to being true to yourself and others. Becoming open and listening to your heart's desires and inner truth and tuning into your feelings, good or bad. Learning to recognise these truths is very important. The ability to express yourself honestly is a key to true authenticity and its good for you. Being honest is not always comfortable as truth often isn't easy to face, however it pays to remember that it serves and is the best road to travel in the end. Being honest with yourself will go a long way to letting go who you are not. Honesty creates freedom, freedom from all kinds of emotional tyrants like guilt and suppression. Truth is a great healer and quite liberating especially when shared for the right reasons. The more you practice being honest the safer you will feel being you, without the need to agree or comply or compromise yourself all the time. This one value would make the world a better place for everyone.

Develop an attitude of happiness:
Learn to cultivate feelings of greater contentment. This acquaints to be satisfied with your self and your achievements no matter how small they might be. When we can become grateful for all opportunities and see joy in all things we find

an inner lightness that keeps us quietly happy and content with moving forward most of the time. We feel content when we share openly the delights of life's journey, when we see and choose to focus on the goodness in all life. Lighten up and smile through the tough times and they too will pass.

Develop an attitude of living consciously in the now:
That acquaints to letting go of the past and healing any schisms that may have developed. You cannot change what has happened, you can only forgive any shortcomings or misgivings and move on. We must learn to roll with the tides of life - we cannot control life to our will and to try to do so breeds arrogances. Moving on from the need to constantly be engaged with ones past, or the future possibilities, means you are free to enjoy being present in the now moment. When we operate consciously in the now moment we remain open to the infinite possibilities life can and often does present in flow with synchronistic events.

Develop a non-judgmental attitude:
Let go the need to be in control, so stop putting everything into black and white boxes or making things wrong or right - there is a lot of grey in the world. This acquaints to not talking about others in a derogatory way. There is always a reason for everything. A great deal of damage is done when we gossip or talk about others in a judgmental way and this includes yourself. Let go your limited perceptions of what you think is happening in any situation as you will inevitably only see a very small portion of what is going on. Try not to make assessments on fragments of information. Learn instead that everything is as it is meant to be and that everyone is at the right place in the right time for his or her particular karma and learning, even if you do not know what that is. When we let go the need to judge we become more accepting of everything and everyone, we stop stressing about all kinds of silly and often petty things. Learn to accept life's ups and downs as a natural part of the way it is.

Develop an attitude of individuality:
This acquaints to having the courage to be true to yourself and your intelligence, living your creativity and its ideals and goals, allowing it to be expressed as individuality is very important. No two people are the same, respecting this is a key to individualising and feeling safe to be different, to be authentic and

true to who you really are. So dress the way you want, feel how you wish to feel, become your best authentic self. Let your imagination loose and become inspired as an individual. Then let that which inspires grow like a seed inside your spirit, you never know where it might take you or what adventures it will bring. We all have latent and often dormant gifts, talents and abilities and yours are important too. What ever you are is an individualised expression of the one source, god/goddess. We are not meant to be clones of one another, be brave, be bold, be your beautiful real self. Seek and find that which develops your talents and gifts. Discover your authentic life rhythm, its core will be different to everyone else's beat. Just be true to you.

Develop an attitude of success:
This acquaints to not accepting mediocrity as the norm. You see we are all normal folk living a very ordinary existence, but its what we choose to do and to experience that can make our ordinary life extraordinary. Going beyond the norm to find things that challenge and excite us is all part of the need to have success. Success cannot truly be measured by, nor is it about, money or wealth. Success is about living truthfully and fully, experiencing each moment without regret, without shame and without dishonour. Set some goals that will make your heart strive for something and see how it makes you feel to accomplish it. Start with little goals and work up to bigger ones. Make them achievable and keep it real. We should always have things to look forward to and to accomplish in life - it helps us to keep moving forward in our chosen direction. Learn to take small steps at first; Rome wasn't built in a day. Stop along the way and see just how far you have come and enjoy the view from where you are now, knowing the journey you've had to get there. Now give thanks, for the journey is what it's all about. Knowing this is wisdom indeed.

The Goddess & Sisterhood

The mind of a woman is directly linked to her feelings and emotions. So what flows out of her mouth in an intimate conversation with female friends, is likely to be her raw thoughts and feelings. Women have learnt to process their otherwise unattended or heard feelings through conversations with each other, thereby transforming them with the use of the spoken word. Couple that, with the safe, loving and caring supportive energy often generated by a group of gathered girlfriends and you have an unsolicited therapy session for women.

Through nurturing friendships women purge themselves of life's ups and downs. They draw on each other's support as a source of inner strength, which helps them to cope with what life dishes up. What they may not know, however, is that it's good for their inner and outer health and general mental wellbeing. After having shared oneself with female friends, one cant help but feel validated, uplifted, unburdened, lighter, self-realized and not alone. And in case you're wondering if women talk about men or sex. The answer is yes absolutely.

Women love to share all the details of their lives if they feel it's appropriate and safe. They share what worries them, what makes them laugh and brings them joy, they share their triumphs and their sorrow and this allows them to feel it, own it and deal with all that it brings to them. Good or bad is not what this is about, for women generally harbour no judgments as to what is going on in each other's lives, they simply observe. There is an unwritten understanding within the female psyche that accepts one day your up and the other you're down – while tomorrow is another day and you'll feel different yet again. They understand that it's okay to have a bad day or feel neglected or hurt by someone's action or non-action, whatever the case may be. They know that men are a source of continual frustration, amusement and bafflement with their bizarre, often male

Neanderthal and sometimes thoughtless, hurtful behavior.

As a hairdresser of some 18 years I was privy to the inner most workings of the feminine psyche. However, it wasn't until I had left hairdressing and missed the company of women myself, that I realized how important it really was for women to commune with one another. The silent role I had played for years also became known to me, for I realized I kept a sacred woman's temple. Teaching the path of the Goddess to women brought me full circle back into the fold so to speak, and I've never been happier or more content. The sisterhood and gathering of women kind is very important to the healthy psyche of women.

Women need the support and unconditional love that shared feelings gives them. It's a special process that women have developed over eons, as they were often left to raise their babies alone and without emotional support from family or spouses. The female community is an extended family that can and does rally for its own kind. Women nurture women in a way that men never can, or rarely do, and women understand this.

They allow each other to be girls, to do girly things, talk girly talk; express their goddess energy in whatever way is appropriate at the time without judgment. This is a true blessing and one that needs to be encouraged and cultivated in these times of challenge and change. You should have a girlfriend who is affectionate; one you cry with, one you laugh with, one to shop with, one to share secrets with, one that you confess to, one to go out and have fun with, one who counsels you without judgment, one who is wise, one who is boyfriend savvy and one who always tells the ugly truth, no matter what. Sometimes you'll find one or two with more than one of these qualities if you're lucky, but its wise to have a few as this creates a fabulous support system.

The Sisterhood a very important source of support

All too often we become overwhelmed with the demands and pressures that life places upon us with family, work and relationships - to the neglect of our need for female companionship. As we get busy we seem to push them aside or into the background. Many women have expressed to me over the years how they feel swallowed up by their loving relationships and seem to lose that sense of self and often their friends. It seems that the devotion and commitment it takes in giving love to a man and then creating a family equated to leaving everything else behind. Balancing and maintaining that sense of self with the demands of work, love and family are all important. Finding time to be a woman and allowing the goddess in you to be expressed with the help of other women is a great equalizer. Get together often with your friends and make time to cultivate new ones if you feel the need. Quite often our changed attitudes and feelings mean we must move on from some friends and that's okay too. Making new like minded friends is important.

Nurturing the sisterhood means making special regular times to meet and do coffee or lunch or even a night out on the town. Give yourself permission to do this and get a baby sitter for the kids if need be. It's a very healing experience to be able to share truth and love with a close girlfriend. If you're stressed, pick up the phone and talk. Don't be afraid to reach out - she will understand.

Reclaim your sense of self by first allowing yourself to be a woman with girlfriends, talking with them will help you explore what is or isn't working in your life. Friendships often mirror who and where we are in the big scheme of things - mentally, emotionally and spiritually. They help us reflect how we feel about life and ourselves, which helps our awareness understand how to make those needed adjustments or improvements. Of course we decide these things for ourselves, but their input often gives us the encouragement and support we need as we go about changing and growing. It is said that women live longer as a direct result of being able to find solace in their friendships with other women, even into their old age. Having girlfriends helps them stay calmer and more able to cope in times of stress.

So girls make no mistake, it is important that we gather and give ourselves the grace and space to be with each other and forge sincere friendships that nurture us, for we need to talk in the special way that only women can with each other...

Things You Might Like To Do With Sisters:

- Meet regularly once a week for coffee with one or more friends.
- Better still create a coffee morning and gather a few friends at home.
- Car pool as you drop off children at school and do coffee after.
- Have a craft afternoon and make masks or dream catchers, get creative.
- Take up a Pilates class or gym membership together, or join as a group.
- Make time at least once a month to see a new movie with friends.
- Organize a day spa outing and share the fun and girly pampering.
- Be silly and have a good old fashioned girly pajama party.
- Reinvent your wardrobes together, share ideas about revamping your image.
- Share a make up class or teach each other new ways to do your eyes and lips.
- Plan a weekend road trip to get away and unwind without the men.
- Go shopping for some new clothes together – that's always a great idea.
- Join a club you like that can make for social gatherings to meet new friends.
- Hit the town for a girly night out, dance and let your hair down.
- Blow away the cobwebs of life with an overseas trip on a cruise ship.

Unveiling the Dark Goddess

Allowing the natural ebb & flow of life

As a practicing Priestess and Goddess one has to take on the many lessons that are sent as challenges within our life path. These can come in many forms and for various reasons, but all of them gift us with amazing knowledge as we accept what it is we need to be taught. I've observed that they're often found in the things that annoy us and we complain about. Listen to a person long enough and you will hear what is being sent as a Life lesson for them. When things are being mirrored to us in our life, we need to be open to it and to ascertain what it is within ourselves we are seeing that disturbs us, or what it is we are needing to realize about our own nature. This deeper inner work and journey is sacred, it is the transformational work of the Dark Goddess and it must be done and completed to be able to become whole.

She assists us to go deeper into the darker/shadow self, to let go and surrender more of our ego, and just when you thought you had had enough, you soften and she makes us surrender yet again. She works through our judgments of others, through our impatience and lack of natural flow in allowing situations to unfold in their own time. She teaches us to trust life on a whole other level, and cannot be rushed, pushed or manipulated. For she sees all and knows what is perfect for us, and what we are needing to be experiencing. Alas it may not be comfortable or easy, but it is perfect.

The dark goddess is a hard taskmasters and she requires our respect as we allow her processes to work their inner magic on us. She helps us to experience the deeper richer aspects of the life, making us accountable and sometimes uncomfortable for what we feel, think, say and do. She is the keeper of our integrity towards others and ourselves. She makes us forgive and have compassion for things we didn't even notice before, that need our love, understanding, caring and attention. She shows us that life is often messy and awkward and definitely not perfect, and that it cannot be run like a strict timetable of events even if we'd prefer it did.

My personal favourites are those who like control of everything, for they are the ones that seem to bump and grind the most, complaining, constantly about everything. Nothing is right or good enough for these people. They take pleasure in finding fault with just about anything, its a fabulous life drama. But what they are really saying is please don't judge me, please make me feel secure, make my life happy, make me feel okay and make my choices right. They are often in need of love and support and encouragement to experiment with life, as in truth they are afraid of anything different or new. Watch as they fly to defend their opinions and judgments. Sad really the narrowness and inner limitation this has on how they choose to experience life.

Life can be a trickster and just when you thought things were all organized, the dark Goddess comes along to mess up your plans. Don't you just love how that happens!? Age and wisdom makes us adept at this, so we flow and immediately look for new solutions. There's no point worrying about it or making molehills into mountains, reacting or resisting the obvious. This types of life lesson is simple really, albeit hard for us to comprehend and understand at the time. The learning is often subtle in its awakening, but can be harsh in its effect upon us. We can react in the moment, needing time to sit back, reflect and process how we were disappointed and why. What was our attachment, and why had we made this more important than anything else. We must look for the gem, the gift of the actual moment, rather than be caught up in not being in control, or being right, and be able to remain humble in our human embodiment, accepting the sacredness of our inner surrender and learning curve.

The Wisdom of the Dark Goddess

To be able to benefit from her wise counsel one must first get into real flow with everything, but especially with self, and this means knowing yourself. Being clear about your truths and listening to your own emotional rhythms. She helps us to know when our energy is high and when its not. She knows its important for us to stop and go within for silence and rest, for self connection and inner reflection. Knowing when to stop and step back and accept that things may be out of balance, or are not flowing properly is important.

The Dark Goddess helps us see that anything we are wanting to have happen, we must surrender and let go of how it happens and allow it to come to us if it is in our highest good. She often sends us the opposite to what we are wanting to make us really look at our need or desire in depth reassessing its true value.

"Are you sure this is what you are truly needing now?"

She makes us look at our wilfulness, our need to dictate an outcome through control or emotional manipulation of others or a situation. Most of the secrets to success training I see out there in the world, is all about getting what you want with very little emphasis placed on 'is this in our highest good to be experiencing'. It seems to focus on the desire and control mechanics for the outcome. If I can dream it I can have it! Can we? Is it that simple?

I do not think so. I have found it's often far more complicated than that, and has much more effect when we surrender to the universe and allow it to have a hand in our destiny. For this to take place we must let go control and get into real flow within and without! We must observe ourselves and notice subtle things.

The dark goddess helps us strip away our falsehoods and get real. She helps the naked truth of things to surface, the core of who we are; our mind, body, emotions, and spirit. She insists that we live from this place of truth constantly without reservation. And trust me, your conviction to live this truth and natural dynamics in you life will be tested! You must be clear about it and know it is the natural law of the universe flowing through your life. So expect some melt downs!

This must become a way of being, not becoming. It is about realizing that in the moment things can and often do change without notice. That even though you wanted to go see someone at a specific time or day, that the timing may not be right and therefore the meeting doesn't take place when you think it is going to. Or that you want to go somewhere but in fact the universe has other plans for you that day. Remaining in flow allows for this, without feeling wrong or bad or judged. If you get into real flow, what you will find is those that are not in flow with you will be removed from you life, because they are not in sync with you or your process and therefore will not flow with it. This is happening all the time albeit as a subtle life undercurrent, never the less it is in process constantly. Those that realize this feel its flow and accept it as being real. Synchronistic events and chance meetings happen all the time for those who are not in control, but who flow and are in contact with the rhythm of their own energies and life.

When you engage this flow, your intuition is connected to the cosmos and the soul planes of reality become manifest in your life. You get real thoughts about going somewhere, because it feels right, you meet a special person, or have an amazing encounter or experience. This is the dance of life that cannot be seen, it is the magic of the universe as it dances between the spaces in timeless existence, as it has for eons. Learn to let go and wait for signs for the next step, for the next clue to your ever unfolding destiny.

The magic of the Dark Goddess

She exists in the Void, in the darkness of time and space, in nothingness, where all possibilities are made manifest. In her darkness is a comfort, a sense of all expansiveness, all allowing, in forgetting and forgiving, a sense of acceptance and vastness. This is the scary openness of the Dark Goddess, she has no limitation, no plan, she is organic, she is accepting of all without judgment, she allows everything and is just a place of creation. She is death and birth and all that is in between, she is dwells in the unknown, the infinite universal expression, the void of omniscience of oneness. She is open yet hidden, dark and mysterious, she is the veiled possibilities that lurks in the unknowable, waiting for you to experience her.

She is the underworld of our subconscious mind, where all that we want to hide is kept, our secrets, our fears, our anxieties, our betrayals, our jealousies and resentments… a melting pot of unforgiveness that must be travailed before wholeness can be a comforting place. Those who have pathworked themselves understand their darkness and have reconciled themselves with it. Once your darkness is known to you and you are comfortable with this part of yourself, you will find you will fear it less in others, but you will be able to spot it, call it out and expose it easier. That is the gift of the dark goddess, for once revealed you cannot go back into denial of what is, you can pretend if you like, but it will not serve you anymore.

Take control, claim your power & change your life!

Dancing with your Shadow

For many years now I have been working with and seeing the shadow side or darker nature of people as a psychic therapist. The dark Goddesses take us on an inner journey, enhancing our understanding of how this intrinsic part of our deeper subconscious lunar nature works. For many years I have been pointing out how her lessons from this can and do serve us. As we observe each other and ourselves, we gain insight as to how the shadow is dancing in our lives. Assisting clients often meant pointing out how this part of their nature was acting as a catalyst for their current negative experiences. There are many tell tale signs as to how our nature lets this part of us serve our personal growth. It's through our negative trials and tribulations in life that we learn about how we can over come great obstacles, within and without! On the road to greater self-awareness we must learn to understand our shadow, our darker self, so that we become aware of how we betray ourselves, as well as honour ourselves, enabling the experience of the totality of out being. Once understood we can take responsibility for everything, then darkness within can be harnessed and controlled and any lessons from it can be seen clearly. Knowing this part of us helps to bring about wholeness.

Our Fears and anxieties are the biggest portals to experience the shadow self.

Each anxiety has the potential for us to develop all kinds of mild psychotic behaviours, while we discover the inns and out of how it plays with us on many levels. Dancing with the shadow means just that … you have to allow it to mirror an aspect of yourself until you get to understand what it is demanding you overcome. The mirrored effect is intense and dynamic and allows you to see yourself reflected through a circumstance or another person's behaviour. Here is a clue… "What we resist, persists." Yes… This is especially true with regard to fears and anxieties. So, whatever you fear the most and focus on the most will be amplified and so is attracted to you in some form. The harder you try to avoid it, or resist it, the more you bring it on. Sounds' strange doesn't it, but it's not really. It's the law of attraction in reverse. You see the universal delivery clerk doesn't discriminate or judge as to what you place your focus on, or need delivering. It simply responds to your mental/emotional focus, by delivering its required experience. Cosmically ordered by you in complete service to you.

What you focus on is amplified and attracts attention.

Notice what you are focussed on! If your focus is on any fear, doubt or anxiety enough or you are always trying to avoid them, guess what? You will attract them! Yes it's true!
Here are just a few examples of fears or phobias: fear of… not being liked or loved, being alone, left in the dark, lack of money, being too fat, being ugly, having no friends, going unnoticed, success, being unclean, claustrophobia, not being good enough, not achieving an outcome, speaking out, water or drowning, fire or flames, crowds, flying, heights, spiders, snakes, intimacy or sex, loss, death, persecution etc… and the list goes on.

Write a personal list of any fears or little phobias you have or had, and you'll see what I mean. The trick is to learn to observe how your reactions or resistances are triggered while trying to avoid them. What avoidance strategies or techniques have you developed? What does it tell you about you? How does your fear feel? What emotions are you experiencing? Notice your body-mind signals, what are your physiological symptoms? (i.e. shallow breathing, speeding up of heart rate, sweating, tightening or twitching of muscles etc). These are your physical stressor signs. Start to notice your signals, and then start to pull back, relax and breathe… Allow yourself time to learn and observe all these things.
The trick to over coming our dark side is to face what we fear and come to realise it only has power over us if we allow it. Notice why you feel disempowered by it, what insecurities it triggers, what stories you make up to avoid confronting the truth about your fear. Let go of the need to feel disempowered by it constantly.

What is it trying to tell you about you? How can facing it help you to grow, what is needing to be developed by experiencing it. Look for the positive in the challenge of it. Everything happens for a reason. Become a fear detective and look for clues as to why you are experiencing it. There is always an upside that creates the balance. Once you are prepared to face the inner wisdom from experiencing the fear, conquering and letting it go will become easier.

1. Anything we have a negative reaction to has power over us.
Whenever we react negatively we are connecting to a part of the inner self that either feels vulnerable or insecure, frightened or angry. Often this sensation comes from a perception of loss, possibly of control over some part of life or the self. A reaction can take many varied forms, mental, emotional or physical: like withdrawal, shutting down, talking fast, or constantly chattering, justifying, feeling guilty, feeling wrong, abandoned, lonely, lost, wounded, anger or rage, or agitated and frustration, disappointed or hurt. We may start sweating, become quiet, our teeth may start chatting or we experience shivering or shaking or crying or yelling. When we can overcome a reaction when we have conquered an aspect of the unknown self and regained our sense of control over our personal power. First acknowledge the reaction and the emotions it generates, listen to its wisdom. What is it telling you about yourself? What have you really reacted to? Why has it upset you? How important is this on a scale to 1-10? Is your reaction helping or adding to your life right now? Are you creating a drama for attention? Be honest with yourself as to your real motives and reactions. In this way you can observe your reactions and then slowly start to take control, breathe and let them go, relaxing back into and trusting the flow of life. The minute you do that you take back your power, stay calmer and can deal with what ever is unfolding much easier.

2. Attachment to an outcome can become an anxiety, leading to mild paranoia… (the fear of it not happening.)
The mind races with inner questions, fearing the unknown, what that might mean, the circumstances it might bring if something we want doesn't happen. We often begin things with an outcome or desired result in mind, like setting a goal. But the minute we make it an obsession or 'have to have', it becomes a portal to experience loss and disappointment. We can spend a lot of time developing all sorts of control behaviours to avoid disappointment. The best

thing to do is to set a goal, but then let go attachment as you work towards it. Trust that if you are doing everything possible to bring it about then the universe will eventually deliver it, in the way that is perfect for you. "What you are seeking is also seeking you!" … It's just a matter of time. Let go and let it come to you in perfect timing.

3 Whenever you give your power away through non verbal agreement, either by not speaking your truth, or pleasing people.

This is harder to spot, as often we are simply trying to keep the peace, be nice, amiable and polite. But in doing so we can often be seduced into nonverbal agreement… that is agreement by omission. When we don't say yes but choose instead to say nothing because we are afraid to offend by saying no. In that moment it can be assumed that we are in fact in acceptance of and therefore in agreement, because we haven't voiced our thoughts or actually stated our objections in any form. Especially by those who are seeking your agreement. This is of course a subtle form of manipulation, which happens all too often. Good-natured people can be taken advantage of, and are often coerced into agreement like this, without realising it and even be made feel guilty like they did in fact agree by default. Setting boundaries is healthy and will put an end to this type of coercion. Often we need time to think about things so learn to have some phrases at hand to put off any agreement before you have had time to reflect. You could say something like "thanks for you kind offer, but I need to check my dairy" or simply be honest and say "can I have time to think about it and get back to you later?" Accept that you have a soft, polite and kind nature by observing your agreeable temperament, now work on being more specific and set some verbal boundaries by saying 'no' to things… you will gain strength slowly as your personal power and confidence grows.

4 Other people's fears can act as a portal for negative energy to attack you also. If you're around someone who is overly emotional or who suffers anxiety, paranoia, or has anger issues, or an addictive personality, then expect to be drawn into their drama and suffer the consequences. When you choose not to be surrounded by people who suffer these types of influences you can say goodbye to how they would otherwise effect your life. We can develop all sorts of behaviours to help cope with this sort of thing. If you are experiencing circumstances of this nature, you do have options;

a) Stay and get support and counselling to help you cope while dealing with it.
b) Leave and get help to debrief you and re adjust back to your normal self.
c) Stay and learn how best to deal with these types of emotional people.
d) Remove yourself immediately if you think your being abused or your physical, mental or emotional health is possibly in jeopardy.

Unless you have some trained skills dealing with people with disorders I suggest; you stop trying to rescuing people yourself, and get real help or just remove yourself entirely. We are not responsible for other people's behaviours or problems unless we choose to be. Think clearly about how they may affect your life long term before getting too involved with them.

The key to dancing with your shadow is to understand your own emotional nature, how it can be triggered and how it reacts to those triggers. Reaction and resistance are friends of denial I found. Remember anything that pushes your buttons has a lesson in it for you. Note your behaviour, understand what are your triggers, choose new and different responses, shift focus and take better control over your dark side. It's all about the choices we make.

Part Two
Exploring your Inner Priestess

Priestess keepers of the Goddess

"Women who choose to walk the path of the Priestess are serving the higher spiritual ideals of the Sacred Feminine. They are Holy Women, who are dedicated to serving the Goddess!"

The growing need for many of us to connect with this time immortal aspect of the Goddess, bringing back her balance and wholeness, has seen a rise in 'Priestesses' and their sacred spiritual practices the world over.
Though not exclusive to just women, whose dynamic arts are feminine by design, it demands the full embodiment of our inner lunar nature, (*the acceptance of which creates the wholeness of self in a divine union*), combining the ancient earthly feminine ways with the cosmic sacred feminine self. Whether you are male or female is irrelevant really, working with this part of your being isn't necessarily gender based. Connecting with your inner Priestess is all about getting deeply entwined into you're sacred (inner) essence that of the divine feminine, allowing yourself to be immersed in her initiations and sacred time honoured rituals. Many Priestesses hold temple, by that I mean they are teachers, counsellors and healers, running circles sharing the Sacred Feminine in what ever way they can, guided by their inner Goddess, spirit guides and Goddess peers.
The world has become bereft of the Goddess and out of balance, because male energy continues to dominate and run amuck! No wonder the pendulum has swung back towards its polar opposite 'the Divine Feminine'. Connecting with the 'Priestess' part of self brings divine eloquence and helps to quantum leap humanities consciousness into a better more balance understanding.

Becoming a Priestess empowers women to develop individually and creatively, to live their own lives, taking back the responsibility of their Soul's path, which is our feminine birthright, inspiring ones full potential as a living Goddess.

For eons women were treated, as a mundane part of life, excluded not included, resulting in the sacred feminine being suppressed, spoken over, dictated to, raped, pillaged and used for procreation without concern for her wellbeing. However, everything must be birthed and therefore comes through her and everything must go back to her in the end, a fact many have forgotten.

Unlike the worship of the Gods' who were seen as external celestial beings that lived outside of mankind… The Goddess is an integral part of our sacred earthly selves, residing in our awakened state as cocreator of life. The Goddess is in divine partnership with the God and is his consort. Without the goddess and his sexual desire for her there would be no human race living upon this earth. Therefore both must co-create to pro-create. Her forces reside in our instinctual nature, our sexual desire, our emotional tides, and she takes care of our earthly needs, that of comfort, food and shelter, of feeling at home in our environment, of living in balance with our playground mother Earth. Without this conscious connection to her we cannot relate to each other, our birth place or parents, or journey through our earthwalk, we would become bereft, lost of identity without need for community or purpose within it. Priestesses honour this and therefore worship the Goddess as holy women and keepers of her ancient traditions, a bit like priests who keep a church.

Connecting with the Goddess

The first place to look to connect with the 'Priestess' is through the Goddess in Mother Nature. Go out into her deepest forests; let the sweet smell of her trees caress you as they transmute pure oxygen, learn to breathe her sacred air, our most precious life force that connects all living things. Visit that place where that which has died is re-birthed through her organic processes of decaying soil, morphing back, feeding the living once again. Swim in the vast oceans filled with life, surf her tides and play in her waves. Honour your planet and revere her sacred groves and mountains and the fury four legged's that freely roam upon her. See the abundant way the seasons bring the growth of our fruits, veggies and grains for us to be nourished. Note the weather patterns and how she changes the cycles. Observe her rains, filling the rivers, flooding the plains, purifying and washing our bodies. Marvel at the moon and stars in her midnight skies, and let their hidden secrets be revealed to you. Learn her cosmic patterns and let her magic weave their sacredness into your life. Seek and enjoy the means that would open all these ancient time honoured vistas of wondrous knowledge, revealing her best-kept secrets to your mind. Bask in the glory of the time immortal circle of life that are truly her domain. Once open and revealed to you, your life is forever wrapped in a quiet sacred Holiness that is often felt by others intuitively as being special.

Your Ebb and Flow

Every month women menstruate as their female cycle connects with its time-honoured ritual, which helps to procreate our species. While no fan fare plays a tune as this happens, it should be noted and respected as being a fundamental Divine Feminine Cycle of life. This release of cyclic creative womb blood from the Goddess is what we all suckle from in the begging of life, it is sacred and should be respected and honoured in a sacred way. Connecting with this cyclic part of the feminine helps to respect her ability to gestate (and create) life, one of the most magical creative and feminine life forces we have. As a Priestess honouring your moon time, (*menstruation*) is part of respecting your connection to the inner Goddess. Observe and learn about your own inner emotional tides, this will help you connect with your moon/lunar nature, (*how you are guided emotionally throughout your cycle*) once you have a better understanding of this aspect of the self, you will come to see how this is reflected in via your rhythm's throughout your day to day life. Many women menstruate in alignment with the full moon. Menstrual blood holds the highest vibration connected to the earth Goddess with in you and should be treated with respect. Calling it the "curse" or worse does not honour its life giving essence, for none of us can be birthed without it. Learn to love this part of your sacred femininity for it is a true blessing. Some Priestesses collect this blood of the goddess by rinsing out pads in a bucket of water, blessing the water, and ritually sprinkling it over the garden nourishing mother earth as a sacred offering to the flower and devic kingdom.

Set up your Goddess Alter

Every priestess needs to have a focal point for her sacred practice and that point is usually her alter. An alter is a symbolic sacred place that is used to connect with, reflect, give thanks and manifest through the Divine. It should reflect the way you see the divine feminine, (*what is holy to you*) as a place to worship your higher principals and observe her rituals in a realistic changing if not in an organic way. It can show the season/cycle of the year, the particular feminine deity you maybe needing to work with. The use of vegetation, such as plants or flowers, food or offerings makes for great symbolic representation of the seasons, joyful abundance and our ability to receive nourishment from her through our life giving planet earth or Gaia.

As do any of the Elements such as wands or candles for fire, shells or goblets for Water, crystals or pentagrams for Earth, ornate feathers or carved bejewelled dagger's for Air. The use of burning incense, ringing of chimes or bells for the summoning of spirit also helps create a sense of ceremony as one focuses on the divine feminine connection. It can be a shelf, cupboard top or special table placed in a certain position or space. The use of colour is important as it reflects who you are and what you need to express. Change it regularly, keep your alter fresh, it is a spiritual focus after all and should reflect the inner you, who you are, where you come from, and where you are choosing to go now.

Create your personal Sacred Space

Now every Priestess needs to know the practice of how to create sacred space. This is a place either inside or out or both if you like. Often it can be at the same place where your Alter is but not necessarily. I use my alter daily and it is in a common area in view of everyone who walks into my home, but I like to keep my sacred space separate, more private and personal. However, certain rituals require a special alter designed with a singular purpose in mind.

Wherever you choose it must be able to be used without interruption from others, it must be sacred for you and honour your time spent there. Firstly, sweep and spring clean the area, if you can sprinkle it with salt and leave it over night or for a few days that's great. Make sure to get into the corners, nooks and crevices. You can paint it if you like, or hang your favourite Gods & Goddesses in and around the sacred space creating a feeling of reverence.

I grid my sacred space with crystals in a sacred geometric pattern, sometimes I draw it on the floor, or lay it out using crystals as I work the area claiming the space. Make sure there is a space that's kept open in the centre. Here you will create your circle and build up the energy for magickal rituals and ceremonies as you path-work your connection to the divine feminine. Cleanse your space throughout the year especially before ceremonies and rituals of any kind.

Smudging and Cleansing

Once you've created your sacred space take some white sage, lavender or sweet grass and place it in a bowl over a burning charcoal. Let the herby smoke start to rise gently. Using a large turkey or eagle feather or smudging wand, start by gesturing the smoke gently pushing it away from you using the feather/wand, out into every part of your space, make sure you smudge it thoroughly. As I do this I usually call upon the ancients and the Goddess, banishing any negative or dark energies, so that they be removed from this space, leaving only the purity of the divine in its presence. I ask that all those that enter this space be blessed with healing and love from the divine Goddess, so that only truth and love shall be its intent. After smudging I sprinkle rose water or lavender water to wash the area again. Leave all doors and windows open to let pure air bless and cleanse all smoke out. Over the entrance I hang fresh herbs of basil, rosemary, thyme and lavender to ward out negativity and bring good luck and positive energy forth. Each season I change the herbs and use different ones. You can adopt whatever practices you see fit in your own space that maintains its sacred value for you. Again regular smudging is recommended, in fact I usually smudge every ritual and ceremony and everyone that enters my sacred space. It is a sacred time honoured ancient ritual that's used to protect and watch over all that takes place.

Aligning with the natural Elements

Attuning oneself to the natural rhythms of mother nature's Elements is essential in shamanic healing, magical work, or Priestess practices. Each has its own symbolism and activates certain realms within us that can be used in pathworking, ceremonies and rituals, spellcraft and meditations. The elements make up all the main alchemical ingredients of mankind and our world, therefore each embodies aspects of our human process either, mental, emotional, physical and spiritual. Each element is said to be peopled by spirits and mythological entities called elemental's or nature spirits. All elements correspond to a particular direction, North, East, South or West, which are called the Quarters in circle work. Each quarter has it's own Archangel called a Guardian. As you start to work with the elements you become more attuned to their energy and have a better understanding of that which is represented by this within yourself.

▽
♉ ♍ ♑ *Earth - Physical - North - Archangel Uriel*
Earth is the element of stability, foundations and of the body. The Earth is the realm of wisdom, knowledge, strength, growth and prosperity. It is also the physical Earth on which we live and the very heart of life. It is essential in spells and rituals of prosperity, business, fertility and stability. Earth is a feminine element.

△
♊ ♎ ♒ *Air - Thoughts - East - Archangel Gabriel*
Air is the higher mind element. Find a place with clean air and breathe deeply, touch a feather or inhale the fragrance of a heavily scented flower. In magickal terms, Air is the power of the mind, the forces of intellect, inspiration, ideas & imagination. Air can be both Masculine and Feminine, depending on how it is used. It's creative and intuitive force is Feminine, but it's planning or carrying out, step by step logical force is Masculine.

△
♈ ♌ ♐ *Fire - Actions - South - Archangel Michael*
Fire is a masculine element, its aspects being change, passion, creativity, motivation, will power, drive and sensuality. It is sexuality, both physical and spiritual. Fire is used in spell casting, rituals and candle magick for healing, purification, change & transformation, sex, breaking bad habits or destroying illness and disease.

▽
♋ ♏ ♓ *Water - Feelings - West - Archangel Rafael*
Water is a cleansing, healing, psychic, and loving element. It is the feeling of friendship and love the pours over us when we are with our family, friends and loved ones. When we swim it is water that supports us, when we are thirsty, it is water the quenches our thirst, another manifestation of this element is the rains that falls and the dew that forms. Water is a feminine element.

⊙ *Spirit - Aether - All that Is - God & Goddess*
Spirit is the fifth element, the binding energy that runs through all matter, and it is also the collective unconscious of every life-form. We are all made of this and therefore we can all connect at this level! We experience it as our energy or the intrinsic life force of all living things. It is the source of our life force!

Serpent Rising: the Purification

As a young priestess initiate, I realised there was a deep transformational process of purification, of letting go, transmuting ones lower nature with the will of the higher mind. I had to learn to willingly use certain disciplines and practices. With regular use of pranic breathing, meditations, and energetic techniques, I began making inner adjustments to my lower nature (ego self) through these practices. Over time one can became an adept at the spiritual process of inner purification. Some say this is not for the feint hearted, and I must admit that embarking on this inner journey was not altogether a conscious experience for me initially. I was dragged kicking and screaming most of the way whilst dealing with my resistances... (*it was most undignified.*) However, as I progressed I found that the inner self (soul) takes over as one awakens and stimulates that deeper need within to evolve. I noticed there was a natural quickening that organically takes place as one enters this spiritual process of journeying through specific levels of inner purification. These techniques can be found as part of any Shamanic journey, and other eastern Yogic practices.

Rising the Serpent (*otherwise known as the Kundalini*) takes time and patience as well as great discipline. It involves opening up your energy centres (chakras), working the spiritual energy through them, applying rigorous meditations, (higher mental) practices to awaken each Chakra, accessing the consciousness found within, dispelling the lower ego lessons that need to be learnt and understood, which all takes time, patience and diligence to master. First one must become energy conscious, become aware of oneself and ones environment, including people, places and situations in many varied and subtle ways. Once you are able to feel and sense or intuit things you take responsibility for how you react and or respond to them. You become conscious, awake and therefore better able to cope and handle life. You are able to wield energy, co-create and manifest exactly what you want and need, you learn to dance with the universe. The process of 'Kundalini Awakening' is not only one of awakening one's spiritual energy, but also of bringing it upwards, through each of the chakras. The techniques using body, breath work, and mental focus, have various effects on these centres, and pave the way for the 'Kundalini Rising' to move further upward over time. As the energy moves up it has the effect of purifying oneself. The initial awakening and preparation purification takes you through your two base chakra's lessons of individuation from family tribe and primal activities, mastering of all our base physical desires. Including the stimulation of our fight or flight self preservation of self mechanism in many trying life situations.

Each Chakra has within its consciousness both negative & positive attributes, that are triggered with our personal life lessons and chosen karma. A word about karma;- we all have this, wether we believe it or not, we must complete a certain amount in every lifetime as we evolve our soul throughout time and space. This is a sacred journey that takes courage, compassion and much discipline. Those of who undertake it again eventually become teachers of it in other lives. I became a teacher in this life again and feel quite honoured to do so.

About your Chakras

The word chakra is a Sanskrit word meaning 'Wheel of Light' and is the unseen energy centre within the 'etheric' auric field/body. These centres act like our energies intake and ex-take organs, like a plumbing system, used to ensure and stimulate our health, vitality and, ultimately, enlightenment when fully activated. Mystics describe a set of energy centres called Sefirot, that can be seen as the refined spiritual centres on the cabalistic Tree of Life, which can also be matched with points of the physical body. Buddhism, Sufism, Taoist Yoga and Tantric traditions all believe in degrees of this concept. In their individual practices, all these traditions encouraged gradual spiritual development with the belief that each chakra centre will open up more as the initiate matures spiritually. These chakras function within three general groups of processes, with a predominance of the three primal elements, they are:

1. Base-Tamas

The first two chakras relate to the primal activities that operate in relation to the physical world, including the drives for self-preservation and procreation, effectively obscuring higher experience.

The Base Chakra connects us to the core of mother earth and therefore relates to our will to live and supplies the body with physical vitality. Which in turn supplies energy to the spinal column, the adrenal glands, and the kidneys. This is where we integrate our fears and the will to live. Governs the amount of life-force energy an individual can sustain, and functions as action and the receiving of pleasure. Its element is Earth and vibrates as the colour RED. If this chakra is blocked or underactive the person will not make a strong impression in the physical world. They will avoid physical activity, will be low in energy and may even be sickly. It leads to lacking of physical strength. All our basic instincts for survival are latent within the consciousness of this chakra. It deals with our family-tibal connections, and in times of crisis it activates the fight and flight mechanism. An overactive base chakra may result in one being very physically oriented, competitive, sporty, or can make them aggressive or prone to fits of anger or rage. Regular connection with nature and physical activity will help it keep balanced.

The Sacral Chakra is located above the pubic bone beneath the naval. It is the centre of the sacrum, which governs the emotional life of the individual. It is related to our sensuality and sexuality. In women this centre is within the womb, and in men it is called the 'will' point and centred in the gonads. It governs the quantity of sexual energy. It sends energy to the immune system and helps us with our use of sex and food. The seat of our creative self it helps us express our emotions in a creative manner. Its element is Water and vibrates as the colour ORANGE. If this chakra is blocked it leads to malfunctioning emotional and sexual energy, resulting in tendencies to either avoid or over indulge in sexual pleasure. Issues of closeness through the sexual communion or intimacy with another are dealt with here. Understanding our emotional lives becomes paramount, and Deep-seated emotional issues or behaviour can be brought back into balance through the consciousness of this centre.

2. *Heart-Rajas*

The third and fourth chakras, the navel and the heart centres, involve a subtler relationship with the world, working with one's individuality rather than just engaging the physical world.

The Solar Plexus Chakra connects with the stomach in the body. It supplies the stomach and all related digestive organs such as liver, gall bladder, pancreas, spleen, and nervous system with energy. It is associated with our mind processes and is related to who we are in the universe and how we interact with others and take care of ourselves. It regulates our emotional life and human connectedness. We show sympathy/empathy, our desires and aspirations. Its element is fire and vibrates as the colour YELLOW. If this centre is blocked we feel disconnected from the universe and feel lost, not belonging anywhere. Feelings become unbalanced and the ability to be able to feel sensations, emotions, energy, etc., is an issue within this chakra. One will not be aware of a deeper meaning to life and not be able to understand an individual's uniqueness within the universe. Personal power becomes unbalanced. We become more apathetic towards our physical health. Developing a sense of how we feel in relation to and with others are all part of the consciousness of this chakra.

The Heart Chakra is in the middle of the chest and is the centre of spiritual awakening. Those who fully awaken the heart chakra have incredible experiences. It governs the ability for humans to give and receive love while learning about unconditional love. This is where we relate best to nature – our link with physical reality. It supplies energy to our heart, circulatory system, thymus, vagus nerve and upper back. Its element is air and vibrates as the colour GREEN. If this centre is blocked there will be a lack of self love or an increase in selfishness. A person will have trouble loving, or giving without expecting anything in return. There will be an overwhelming sense of non-connectedness with all fellow humans and with all life. People can try to own their mate or person they love. They may lack trust in their life and be quite fearful. Soul awareness and our role in the universe can be stimulated through developing the consciousness of this chakra.

3. *Third eye–Sattva*

The fifth and sixth chakras, the throat and the eyebrow centers, begin movement away from the outer towards the inner world of purity, intuition, creativity, and wisdom, from which the outer arises. Three knots or granthis are broken: Along the Kundalini channel there are three knots (granthis) of energy that will be broken or untied along the upward journey of Kundalini Rising, allowing the flow to go into and through the various chakras above that point:

The Fifth Chakra is located in the front and back of the throat. It is associated with the senses of hearing, tasting and smelling. It supplies energy to the thyroid, the bronchi, lungs and alimentary canal. It is where mental creativity takes place with planning and scheming. It governs the power of speech and sound and the ability of the individual to express themselves. It is where we manifest and create on the physical plane. Vibrates as the colour BLUE. When this centre is blocked we blame everything and everyone else for the wrongs in our life. There will be a lack of personal responsibility towards self and others. Our fears become manifested through negative thoughts and actions. Like attracts like. There will be an inability to express thoughts, feelings and desires through speech, writing or sound (music). Trusting life is a big issue here. Pride and a lack of self-esteem are affected and how one sees oneself in society. Fulfilment and success will be difficult to obtain. Bringing what you desire to have happen in your life is manifested into reality via this chakra.

The Sixth Chakra often called the third eye, is located in the middle of the forehead, both front and back of the head. Awakening this centre increases our psychic abilities and intuitive thoughts. It supplies energy to our pituitary gland, lower brain, left eye, nose, ears and nervous system. It is associated with our sense of sight and sense of time and space. It is directly related to our conceptual understanding and the carrying out of our ideas, step by step, to accomplish them. Vibrates as the colour VIOLET. If this centre is blocked then a confused state of mind is common along with the inability to conceptualise ideas (create plans). Compulsive lying and even criminal activity is hatched from this centre. A lack of intuition and or spiritual integration within the person is usual. An inability to dream may occur also. This chakra develops all aspects of the mind's psyche. Stimulate the consciousness within this chakra and spiritual sight will most likely begin to develop insight and far sight.

4. *Brahma granthi*
Blocking the flow from the first chakra, the root chakra, muladhara, upward to the others; related to bondage to desires.

5. *Vishnu granthi*
Blocking the flow from the third chakra at the navel, manipura, upward to the fourth chakra, anahata, the heart; related to bondage of actions.

6. Rudra granthi

Blocking the flow beyond the sixth chakra between the eyebrows, Ajna chakra, upward towards sahasrara; related to bondage of thoughts (*compared to pure knowing*).

The Crown Chakra is located at the top of the head or crown, located around the pineal gland. It supplies energy to our upper brain and the right eye. It is associated with our experience of direct knowing and is related to the integration of personality with spirituality. This chakra regulates the amount of light an individual can photosynthesise; hence, it controls the amount of 'enlightenment' or 'consciousness' a person can accept. When fully activated it facilitates cosmic consciousness and total integration of mind, emotions, body and spirit in oneness. Regular practices like meditation, reiki and various energy healing can also stimulate and acivate it. Vibrates to the entire colour spectrum, so it is WHITE. If this centre is blocked then one probably does not have an experiential connection to spirituality or have any real the concepts of the God/Goddess as an energy force. Because of this, one would not understand what others are talking about when they speak of their spiritual experiences. Either a lack of faith would exist or a strong dogmatic belief could result also.

It is most common for the awakened Kundalini to rise through the lower chakras, rather than to awaken and arise through all of the chakras, all the way to the crown. Having the Kundalini awaken and even partial Kundalini Rising is an encouraging and inspiring experience. It is also an experience to observe with humility, as the ego can claim ownership of an experience becoming attached and therefore hold up any further advancement. We can spend lifetimes stuck in certain lessons in consciousness.

In most Goddess teachings and Priestess initiations and practices these same inner purifications and spiritual awakenings are demanded, even brought about, simply to expand ones energy field as one learns how to increase its power. Becoming conscious of this process will help us to self regulate our need to purify, purge ourselves, letting go the old to make way for more of the spiritual self to emerge. Many call this the path of the Dark Goddess as it works through the hidden and through ones ego self, washing away ones negative lower vibrations, dealing with ones darkness/shadow self. A great deal is revealed to you as you journey inward and much must be faced and dealt with. It is a hard task master but one must do ones own inner work to progress on any level spiritually. It has the effect of walking up rather large temple steps. The temple being your higher self or soul self. Each step has awarenesses to be obtained and lessons to be learned and mastered. As you attain a new level of consciousness, your mastery over it is then tested to see how far you have actually come. Once mastered that particular initiation is over and therefore you are ready for the next one. It takes many years to even lifetimes for this purification process, it is a continual process of evolvement of distilling oneself and surrendering to the wholeness of your spirit.

The Moon Goddess

Those who walk the path of the Goddess come to understand the Moon is part of her hidden cosmic mysteries. Get to know your Lunar nature by exploring her energy!

In every day in many ways we are blessed by the light of the moon, where her radiant glow is ever present. Since time immortal she has been our silent guide, a gentle force that is constant in our lives. Since a little girl I was always drawn to her majestic powers, and felt a kind of reverence, as I stood bathed in her soft moonlight. Whenever I could I'd go outside in the full moon and just look up at her in wonder. Little did I know that I was under the spell of the Moon Goddess.

Held in her moon-beam arms, I felt safe and nurtured in a way that, at the time, I wasn't really aware at first. It wasn't till much later in my life that I came to understand how her silent power called and flowed through me, and to all those who are also drawn to her. She is the Initiatrix of the Lunar Goddess and as such bestows her Initiations on those who ask her. These are especially felt by women (mainly during their menstruations or moon-time at first) but they are also felt by some men. However, everyone on the planet is touched by her beauty and presence in some form, wether they are conscious of it or not. Such is the gentleness and sacred way of her radiant permeation; for there is a natural awakening that occurs deep within our coded DNA.

Discovering her activations is an exciting time, as one becomes more conscious of her power and begins the journey into the deeper sides of self.

The Moon awakens our subconscious to be experienced in many forms, and activates our awareness of ebb and flow, all that is dormant and hidden deep within us as Goddesses. During the course of some of these activations she opens up our Third Eye for us to receive messages from spirits, so we can experience the natural gifts of our intuition or inner-sight, that of far-sight and insight. She also activates our natural Lunar cycles of initiations which there are many.

Each lunar initiation can take up to 7-9 years to fully complete before the next one begins its cycle. These initiations bring revelations as to our greater being broadening our understanding of self. We often experience a deepening of our emotions and a heightened sensitivity within all of our senses. It can be hard to explain, but these are natural occurrences' that cannot be avoided on the human journey to spiritual wholeness. It's our birthright to experience them as many are interwoven into the DNA memory and felt in our bodies nervous system and relate directly to our hormones and their times of transition.

The Moon exacts a powerful pull on our world, is earth's only satellite, and reflects the light and energy of the sun. Her presence governs the tides and she influences many of our physical rhythms in the same way. Needless to say the moon has a great effect upon us. Much of how we feel emotionally has to do with where the moon is in our life. For Lunar Activation purposes we try to use her energy wisely. Certain times of the moon's phases are better used for some rituals, spells or ceremonies than others.

A moon calendar is an essential tool when you begin to align with her energies and start to work an alter or plan rituals. By consulting a moon calendar you will effectively start to bring her powerful wisdom into your life.

New Moon

This is a great time to begin things, for renewal and Rituals for growth as the new moon's energy is usually used for the start of something. This time is representative of the maiden phase of the triple goddess. Call upon her to help you at this time.

Waxing Moon

A waxing moon is when the moon is progressing toward full moon and is so gaining power. This can bring increase towards you or attract something to you. It's a great time to make a charm or cast a spell requiring the fulfilment of a request

Waning Moon

Is when the moon's illumination has decreased after full moon, so her energy is being drawn inside and can be stored for later use. This is a good time to cast resolution spells or Ritual for something to be concluded or expelled.

Full Moon

This is when she is at the height of her strength and making magic is easier. Your psychic abilities are usually stronger. It's a great time to manifest a new goal or something you truly desire. Each full moon is different by nature, so it's a good idea to look up the qualities it will have before making any plans for it's Ritual use. Needless to say, just holding a ceremony to honour her presence will bring great satisfaction to any Goddess.

Dark or New Moon

This phase is felt to be a time of caution by magic users - as the power of the moon is strong but internalised and unpredictable. I feel it is a great time for inner transformational work as it helps to deal with the deeper psyche. Call upon the wisdom of the Dark Goddesses, and be guided.

Moonlight Magic

The sun warms with a brilliant ray, but the moon enchants. Lunar's soft blue glow takes away the day's glare and invites rest and relaxation. To invite that power into your home open your curtains and blinds on a full moon and let its glow bathe the room. Place a crystal bowl of water on a moonlit windowsill. The next day, you can move this moon-infused bowl to another room that does not get the moon's blessing. Helps create great energy for healing rooms.

Ode To the Moon Goddess
'Mother Goddess of Moon and Star
Who rules all planets near and far
Who rules the Earth and all within
Who sets the time our lives begin
Who brings us happiness and mirth
Who gives us value and self worth
We thank you for your presence here
And hold you in our hearts so dear
It pleases us to let you know
we give you leave to come and go...'
Blessings...)O(

by Dorothy Morrison
'Everyday Moon Magic'

How to perform a Full MOON Ritual

This is a time honoured ceremony used by many who worship the Goddess and practice her moon ceremonies and rituals. In the beginning when I first started to connect with the Goddess I performed this ceremony on every full moon. Then I eventually branched out as one does in their practice and began working with other moon cycles and the different energy. It was a powerful time for me as I know it will be for you. Working with this part of the Priestess energy helps awaken those lunar cycles and relevant initiations begin to take place. This ritual is usually done on a full moon of course, when her energy is apparent and she shines her brightest. Start by creating sacred space, preferable outside to be under the moon, by purifying with smudge and a broom sweep. Best to prepare the ritual space during the day so you can see where to place everything. Set out your circle using votive candles in small glass jars or glasses. Be sure to place markers for North (Earth), South (Fire), East (Air) and West (Water), as you go around the circle. A compass will help with this. If you have to do it inside a room of your house, make sure to have cleared the space of furniture. Set up Your Alter in the North facing corner of the space. Place on this all that is relevant for the particular month you are using. Note the yearly seasons, or wether it is connected to any Goddess Sabbatts, Solstices or Equinoxes, by checking your moon calender first. Place a large White candle for the Goddess on the alter, this is specific to her full moon energy, cakes and goblet of wine or juice to drink. Inside the circle centre is the best place to place your cauldron for any spellwork you'd like to perform during your ceremony.

1. Start by Lighting the candle and moon incense, cast the circle starting at the East: call in the four quarters (Elements) and make your invocations to the guardians (Archangels). Walk to the centre of the circle and Bless the space: Saying something like:

I offer up this sacred space in this time at this place
For blessings this night within Divine grace
Cleansed of all darkness used only for light
Here we shall worship the Goddess this night
Please touch this circle with your love
As we summon the Goddess from above

2. Wait until you feel her energy arrive - standing with your arms outstretched and palms up you invite the Mother Goddess into the circle ... Say something like:

Oh Mother Goddess please descend from above,
Touch this circle with your light and love
Bring us your wisdom and bring us your sight
Help us to feel your strength in our hearts this night
Through your generous spirit tonight we seek
To be elevated from our lowly earthly seat
Into the depths of your gracious love
Where we're safe and nurtured from above.

3 Now you perform the Charge of the Goddess in her honour...
Recite the words of the Great Goddess, the dust of whose feet are the hosts of heaven, whose body encircles the universe and shines a light for all...

"I who am the beauty of the green Earth,
The white Moon among the Stars,
And the Mystery of the Waters,
I call upon your soul to arise and come unto Me.
For I am the Soul of Nature, which gives life to the universe.
From Me all things proceed,
And unto Me they must return.
Let My worship be in the heart that rejoices,
For behold - all acts of love and pleasure are My rituals.
Let there be beauty and strength,
Power and compassion,
Honour and humility,
Mirth and reverence within you.
And you who seek to know Me,
Know that your seeking and yearning will avail you not,
Unless you know the Mystery:
For if that which you seek you find not within yourself,
You will never find it without.
For behold, I have been with you from the beginning,
And I am that which is attained at the end of desire."

After the invocation you can perform any magic or spells that are relevant to you at this time. Once they are done, bless the cakes from the alter, then take a bite and pass it on around the circle if there are others in your ritual with a blessed be. Once done, place back on the Alter, now bless the wine or juice, pour into the goblet. Take a drink/sip, then pass it on with a kiss and blessed be to the next person in the circle until the goblet reaches the alter. Now you can either take this time to visit each other whilst in the circle or proceed with the closing part of the ritual. Thank the Goddess for blessing the circle and any magic performed, dismiss the the guardians (Archangels), bid hail and farewell to the quarters (Elements) and release the circle, place some left over cakes and juice outdoors for the wee folk and animals as a further blessings.

Now some of you may not wish to create formal or rigidly follow any such structure, as with all things you have free will and may choose what feels appropriate for you and your Goddess associates. In truth there is no wrong or right way to worship the goddess, I have simply given you a brief outline of a very simple ceremony that can be adapted and changed to suit your requirements. I have included more about rituals and ceremonies and their relevant uses in the following chapter.

The use of Rituals & Ceremonies

Having run circles for many years as a practicing priestess of the Goddess I used rituals and ceremonies to help clients and students integrate change into their lives. When we take part in a ceremony we naturally get caught up in the planning, in the organizing, and the orchestrating of it all. And it's during this preparation we take up the responsibility for the intention of what it is we are about to do. We re-align ourselves mentally, emotionally and spiritually as we perform the physical ceremony. Our intention has a direct effect on our conscious and subconscious mind as we experience the inner awareness and or transformation that it brings to us. While these can often be subtle, they are always profound. Ritual is one of the highlights of being a Priestess! It serves many purposes let me explain why....

- *It re-sanctifies all our auric bodies, mind, emotions and spirit*
- *It reminds us of the joys of life and the divine within all things*
- *It's uplifting, motivating, energising and exhilarating*
- *It connects us with our spiritual self and greater community*
- *It's inspires us to be better people and take wiser actions*
- *It purifies the mind, allowing us to be more positive*
- *It solidifies our connection with the Earth and the Divine*
- *It helps us create more effective magic*

There are other ways to manifest changes in the world. But ritual is one of the most powerful I know.

Ritual speaks to the deeper subconscious and reminds us of our innate connection to the Divine Source which we are all part of and so we act from a deeper place and therefore are affected on many levels. In this way, using ceremony to help embrace change is quite powerful. It can help us to let go of an attachment to a place, a person or situation or the past. It can help us embrace why something has happened and the wisdom that's been afforded us for the experience. It can help us to honour the emotions of change, accept and revere the experience as being a perfect process and appropriate for happening in our lives, regardless of wether we wanted it or not.

Many people struggle with change, they find it scary and often overwhelming. We can feel fine about change when it's something we bring about ourselves, that we have chosen, but sometimes we are not in control of some life experiences, and can find ourselves at the mercy of sudden unexpected changes. We can struggle with why this is happening and feel wronged or angry at being forced into having to make sudden changes we would rather not. We can be caught off guard, unprepared mentally and emotionally because we're not expecting a change to take place.

Accepting these unexpected situations can prove to be difficult. Moving house for instance can be a huge deal for some one who loves where they live and doesn't really want to leave, especially if it has had great sentimental value playing a large part in their personal or family life. We form deep emotional attachments when associations such as having a built a relationship or marriage or raising a family have taken place there. We can grieve and even wallow in our perceptions of loss because we haven't recognised the need to value those experiences, by claiming their greatness and what they have given us. Once we have received this as a blessing, then we can begin to willingly embrace the new life adventure that is beckoning our soul with feelings of openness. I have helped many people move through change emotionally, everything from a death of a loved one, to a relationship breakdown, to a change in career, to accepting closure after divorce, letting go of a home for sale, to moving interstate or country.

Ceremonies and rituals help us to integrate our life experiences allowing the depth of our lives to be recognised and honoured. We can feel connected to what's happening and not separated from it, which helps with our psychological processing on many levels. It is the human part of us that needs this, to be able to make sense of it and understand it spiritually. The ancients knew this, which is why they held a ceremony for the change in seasons, and for the cycles of life, they honoured everything that supported ones life with some form of simple ritual connecting it to the cycles of the sun and moon. They recognised the deeper need within mankind to stay connected to all things, to honour life itself.

Symbols To Use For Change

We can get really creative when it comes to personal ceremonies for change. I find it best that each person use things that are symbolic to them. Anything that represents cycles of life or seasons is good. Things like scissors or knives for cutting ties for letting go work well. Photos are great when working with closure in specific partnership changes, such as divorce or break up. Memorabilia of loved ones for example, jewellery, ornaments, are all important and easy to use. Picking flowers or leaves off shrubs form around your home, taken from every corner are great to use for anything to do with a house. Of course it's a good idea to use elements when calling in the energies to help with whatever you are doing. Below is an example of what I mean.

Letting Go Ceremony *(usually done on a waning moon)*

This is great for letting go or healing the loss of a loved one and is used for moving on. Set aside time and prepare things in advance by laying them out.

What you will need:

- Two bowls of water
- Petals of a favourite flower
- 3 Little floating candles
- Rose quartz crystal
- One large white feather
- One large A1 size sheet of cardboard
- Scissors, glue stick and one piece of ribbon
- Old magazines that you no longer need
- Special pictures and memorabilia that you can paste onto the cardboard.
- Pen & Paper for writing Affirmation

The Ceremony

1. Smudge the chosen area creating a peaceful sacred space.
2. Light the three floating candles in the bowl of water and petals, dedicating them to the Trinity and Wisdom of the Triple Goddess.

3. Invoke the four Quarters & Guardians; Summon the element of Water and Archangel Gabriel - use a bowl filled with water and flowers petals floating on top. Helps recognition of emotions.
4. Summon the element of Fire and Archangel Michael - use a bowl of water with floating lit candles. Transformation of emotional feelings.
5. Summon the element of Earth and Archangel Ureil- use a rose quartz crystal. Healing for the physical heart re-connection with self.
6. Summon the element of Air and Archangel Rafael – use a white feather. Checks your purity of thoughts and intentions.
7. Write a personal affirmation/prayer asking for the blessing of the Divine Mother Goddess to help with your need to release, forgive all and or heal your wounds, to bring reconciliation to your heart regarding your particular matter... *(write about what ever the matter involves, be specific)*...You may like to have a statue of your favourite divine mother (*Mary Magdalene or Quan Yin are great for this kind of inner healing work*) as a Goddess Deity focus. If needing more force call in or use Kali the destroyer.
8. Next sit down and begin to create your Collage of memories in a symbolic representation of the journey that was had.
9. Cut out pictures from the magazines that jump off the pages to you, that speak to your heart about your loss or pain, that can symbolic or remind you of an experience or a time associated with what you're letting go.
10. Take your time, feel your feelings and acknowledge them; this part takes as long as it takes. Do not rush your emotional connection is paramount.
11. When you feel you have enough pictures, arrange them on the cardboard in a symbolic story. There is usually a beginning, a middle and an end. Have some pictures that represent how you would like to be feeling having let go, this helps you seek closure and newness on your journey as you begin moving forward.
12. Start and glue them onto the cardboard and as you do say "thank you and farewell" blessing each memory along the journey.
13. Do this with feelings of love and reverence honouring the journey that has taken place. It can be quite emotional to do this, which is appropriate. Allow yourself to feel everything, anger, humiliation, pain and hurt, whatever crops up.
14. Sit with these feelings and let them pass through you as though observing them, blessing them, forgiving them and everything associated.

15. This is a personal ceremony and usually wouldn't be shared with others.
16. When Collage is finished use the ribbon to hang your collage from the top if desired, by piercing two holes to thread it through and tie it off.
17. Hang Collage up where it can be seen by you for one moon cycle only.
18. Now close the quarters and bid hail and farewell to the guardians.
19. After 1 month's time has passed, ritually take it down and burn it along with the reconciliation affirmation on same waning moon, outside in a clear space as a peace offering, sending the old energies up to the Goddess in smoke is an act of closure. Bury the ashes in the ground. This simple ceremony gives quite a powerful releasing as it uses very strong symbolism. Enjoy..!

Part Three
Basic Goddess Archetypes

Aphrodite
Love, Sensuality & Beauty
Embrace the beautiful & sensual Goddess within & explore the potential of your sexual nature.

Athena
Wisdom, Justice, Truth
Stop procrastinating, trust your truth and listen to it's inner wisdom by taking positive action towards your success.

Cordelia
Play Outdoors, Friendship
Create balance within your lifestyle, outside and enjoy sports, being with friends or mother nature.

Isis
Magic, Divination, Sacred
Create sacred space, set up your alter, as the queen of magic connects you to divinational forces and guidance.

Pathworking the Goddesses

There are way too many Goddesses for me to include them all in this book so I decided to only use a few of the main archetypal Goddesses for you to get the idea and begin your journey to knowing them and to inspire you to go look them up for yourself. I created my own Modern Goddess Oracle cards, originally to help many of my students start to identify aspects of the Goddess within themselves and so we could included them in our rituals as we pathworked and in full moon Goddess circles. They brought a whole new awareness to us all as we started to embody each archetype's amazing energy. Feel free to purchase a set to pathwork with as you embrace the priestess within. We all have unique ways in expressing ourselves and there are many Goddess vibrations that you can identify different aspects of your self with, for example: You may identify with Goddess Athena for your mental and work or career aspects, but identify with Kuan Yin for your emotional aspects, bringing a more sensitive and compassionate aspect to the fore. These two can work quite well and help you balance yourself out. Each brings different strength for you to start to embrace as they help you make adjustments to areas of your life that may not have been functioning well. For example if you have had any feelings of ugliness or I'm not attractive or sexy, or having trouble attracting love into your life, then Aphrodite can help you start to feel those sensual, sexual parts and become comfortable with this, attracting lovers or partners for fun as you explore your more sensual nature. You start to get what I mean now I'm sure. Each archetype brings gifts and challenges to you to embrace and overcome. If you take up there support and inner guidance you will be surprised at the results that can be achieved. Try and journal your time spent with each archetypal Goddess energy and honour all that she brings to you and helps you transform.

The Love Goddess
Aphrodite

Mythology has it, that Aphrodite was created from the happy union of the sea and the sky. Having evolved from an early Italian nature goddess, she became known as bringer of spring blooms and vines, good fortune and victory, a goddess of growth and the beauty of nature.

Aphrodite is described as the goddess of grace, love and beauty and is considered the ruling queen over attractiveness, pleasure and passion. Associated with the planet Venus, she symbolically represents love in all its forms; from pure ideal soul mate love to lustful sexual desire. The myth has it that she rose naked from the sea, the source of all life. Born out of the foam of the ocean, she was carried by the west wind to the shores of Cyprus. There she was discovered by Hoare, who sought favour by showing her to the gods whom she enthralled with her amazing beauty. She became known by many names and was respected as the founder of the Roman people, whose romance with love ('Amore') is displayed everywhere within their culture. Legend has it she took numerous lovers and was not particularly faithful, indulging in many secret assignations all in the name of love. Her hot-blooded love affair with Mars led to many offspring, notably son Eros, Cupid and daughter Harmonia. However, it was the discovery of this affair that led to her eventual ridicule and disapproval from all other gods and goddesses, creating much jealousy.

Aphrodite's Venusian connection saw her give the name 'Venus' to the morning and evening star. 'Venus' is the ruling planet of Taurus and Libra in Astrology. As the goddess of desire, she is the irresistible personification of both the passionate physical and spiritual heart aspects of love. Her mythical story acts as a symbolic reminder of the soul's eternal journey through love via the collective unconscious and its eternity. Aphrodite is an archetypal affirmation of a young woman emerging fully into her femininity, embracing all of her beauty, sexuality and pure goddess energy. As a result, she helps women feel comfortable with their bodies, expressing their sexuality and sensuality, increasing desire and romantic passion. She reminds women not to be afraid of or hide their femininity. When we call upon her goddess energies, she guides us through the stormy and calm waters of love and passion, enhancing pleasures of the senses while navigating the physical and emotional aspects of desire.

She helps us to strengthen long-term relationships by allowing passion to have understanding. Within the duality of love, a partner who has passion for you and understands you, can heal occasional hurts and wounds. This encourages the growth of love toward finding a deeper, more committed and caring space. Lust and desire on their own are useless without real love and understanding. Aphrodite brings growth as we move into more mature love in true relationships. She is often used in rituals of love, so call upon her to aid all matters of the heart. She reminds us that 'love leads the way'. When love is present, the whole world acquires a soft, golden glow, enabling us to have more compassion and forgiveness. It opens the heart to see with the eyes of truth and love. This transcends beyond what only the mortal human mind comprehends. This is the divine essence displayed through the true heart of the goddess.

Goddess of Magic

Isis

Isis is said to be the first known true goddess of Egypt from whom we all originate, and one of the most revered goddesses of the ancient world. She is still one of the most popular and well-known goddesses in the world today. Isis is the most powerful goddess to emerge from the rich tapestry of Egyptian culture, only later being eclipsed by that of Christianity's Mary. Isis was and still is revered and often worshipped as the divine mother-goddess, considered as judge of the dead, sister and faithful consort of Osiris, and dedicated mother of Horus. Genealogically she belonged to the Ennead; daughter of Seb and Nut, sister of Seth.

In the Osiris myths she searched for, retrieved, and reassembled her husband's desiccated body after having been killed and scattered by her brother Seth. This connection saw her proclaimed as goddess of the dead, and of the funeral rights, gifted with the magickal psychic powers of divination (seer), and resurrection (healer) of souls. Isis then impregnated herself from Osiris's body and gave birth to Horus in the swamps of the Nile Delta. Here she raised her son in secret and kept him away from her brother Seth. Much later Horus defeated Seth, becoming the first ruler of a united Egypt. Thereafter Isis, as dedicated mother of Horus, was regarded as protectress of the true Pharaoh's throne.

Isis was considered very powerful as keeper of the throne (she became known by her name and symbol), and was seen as holding the space of the throne, a place for the true seat of all nobility who rule, a very important source of the Pharaoh's balance of power. Henceforth maintaining the knowledge that ultimately all things are born of the goddess, keeping the sacred union of masculine and feminine as the personification of the perfect balance of the yin/yang nature in all things.

Often you will see her dressed with the symbolic headdress of a solar disc between the cow horns on her head. This represents her personality, which was believed to resemble that of the Hathor, goddess of love and gaiety. Mostly she was depicted crowned, with a throne, representing royalty, rulership and nobility, and happily with her boy child Horus sitting on her lap, representing love, motherhood, protectress, and fertility.

As a worshipped deity she had her own priests and therefore a following, many temples were erected in her honour. Her largest was built in the Nile Delta on the Island of Philae, later transferred to the Island of Agilkia in 1975-80. Over the centuries much was done to limit, suppress and even wipe out all Isis worship as it was seen to be of the divine mother-goddess. She was made to appear as queen of all dark magickal practices in an attempt to quell knowledge of, and her influence of, the sacred feminine divine practices. This dishonoured and virtually wiped out psychic abilities being revered as sacred truths.

Isis personifies the ancient mystery school's journey of the initiate's path, through priestess, sorceress and goddess, typifying the awakening of the divine feminine path that is available within all women-kind. With the ability to see all things, she rules the goddess energy to conjure and to make manifest, first visually, then practically. As keeper of magick and all things feminine she helps us develop our latent natural psychic powers, enabling us to see/intuit all possible realities, thus helping guide our course in life, with our hearts at the helm, navigating its often choppy, if not, challenging waters. Isis is known for her loving strengths of healing and compassion and of her heart's endurance and willing ability to heal all manner of ills. She goes beyond earthly matters consulting with the divine for truths of the soul kind. In this way she offers us our truth in a sacred sense, asking us to trust what we feel and see with our heart.

A true mother-goddess, she guides our parental love and aids us to be the best wives and mothers we can be. Raising our children into the nobility of respect and honour, guiding their lives from a divine sacred truth, teaching them that we are indeed all connected and therefore have a responsibility to help each other live well, in honest clean living environments, caring for our communities at large, while protecting that which is sacred to us, all the things we love. Her inner fortitude and power offers us courage and strength of spirit, clarity of understanding, and ultimately true wisdom in our hours of need

Goddess of Earth

Gaia

Mother Nature, Support
Thank the earth Goddess for supporting your daily life with her unconditional bounty.

Gaia's heart is the earth mother of us all, a primeval Goddess offering up her ancient knowledge as gatherer of earth walk wisdom, she is the tree of all life, she is the creator of wholeness. Born out of the cosmos as a resting place for the gods, a physical Eden for their pleasure, she is a living breathing entity. She stands for life and creation with no regard for consequences.

She rules over Mother Nature, which is her garden of joyful abundance, with a dynamic rich diversity of opposites; playful rich yet dark forests, sandy palm lined beaches, treacherous mountain ranges and tempest seas, unruly baron desert plains, tropical islands toped each end with frozen polar ice caps. Mix with that her transformational power of seasons and elements, the cycles of life and death, predator and prey, night and day, wet and dry, hot and cold, male and female, yin and yang, and you have a recipe for an amazing physical journey.

Gaia is the earthly divine feminine who rules our physical life and reconnects us with our true nature. She helps us to understand physical transformation, how to ebb and flow with life through the cycles of the seasons for guidance. As the moon gently affects her tidal rivers and seas, so too this reflects our changing inner moods. Gaia is the goddess who watches over all those spirits who walk on her belly, animal, mineral and vegetable, human and insect alike, none of us are here without her grace. Her beauty is everywhere, her laws are simple; her boundaries plain, for gravity and old age are something none of us can disobey. She checks us with our survival, our body's ability to reproduce with the desire, lust, sexuality and fertility; and our health needing food and nourishment and exercise for vitality; and physical comfort needing nurturing clean living home environments.

Through the four elements Air, Earth, Fire and Water we gain knowledge of a different kind, we come to understand the wholeness of our Earth walk connecting us to our more animalistic instinctual nature and to our ancient ancestral roots. The elements keep all aspects of our Mind, Body, Emotions and Spirit grounded in physical reality in our anima.

Gaia helps us to become more organic in our life, to understand that everything has its right season and that to try to control everything is futile. That we are born from her and will return to her upon our death is very real indeed, a reality that keeps our ego in perfect check.

Hers is a power that should be approached carefully, for everything must answer to her at some time. She asks nothing and gives everything, and is able to reclaim anything mankind does to her with time.

Goddess of fortune
Tyche

Wealth & Abundance
Fortune awaits, as she guides your intelligence in financial matters towards a better flow of wealth & abundance.

To the Greeks, lady luck was Tyche; she bestows prosperity, wealth, and apparently good fortune. She is a powerful Goddess who loves different and unpredictable ways, and permanently offers instructive examples to those who do not expect the incredible changes she can effect. Tyche is one of the Oceanids - from the water and linked to our emotions, but it has also been claimed that she was one of the Moerae, and the most powerful sister of the fates.

Although she was a daughter of Zeus, she was reputed as being quite irresponsible. She preferred to run about juggling a ball than to carry the Cornucopia filled with golden fruit. The first set of dice were found in Tyche's temple perhaps indicating the capriciousness of life and luck and the fickle manner in which she decided the fortunes of mortals.

The Copernican/Newton systems and even the great Einstein's theory of how things are, cannot broach the luck, good or bad, which the Goddess Tyche represents. 'Fortune' has a broader implication than just material wealth. It is also intrinsically connected to the vagaries of fate and the degree of luck one encounters in life. On another plane again, it is also about the growth of our spiritual, physical, mental selves, and how they develop wisdom in the sea of chance, risk, choice, and fate.

Tyche governs a vast realm and holds the keys for the spinners of fate. Not to be an outcast of Fortune is one of the deepest desires of most men and women. Tyche is one of the mightiest divinities when it comes to human affairs; beauty and good reputation, they say, are in Tyche's keeping, and even success in love depends on Fortune. In fact, some believe that most things depend on her, including such cardinal things as destiny, success, health, wealth, power, good marriage, and lovely children to name a few. Even the heads of state in ancient times consulted oracles and mystics who could glimpse future outcomes, to be more prepared for what may come to pass, giving rise to the old saying 'fore-warned is fore-armed'.

Fortune without intelligence leads to ruin, this is one of her harsh lessons. The fate of Fortune can be a cruel lesson for some as all they deem worldly can be ripped away in a moment. People often make the mistake of putting their faith in their material possessions only to lose them in a crisis, uncovering a falsehood in their actual power over them.

It has also been said that gold, repute, health, strength, beauty, and all other gifts of Fortune, need to be commanded by a person's intelligence. For through this intelligence and our moral purpose, we are able to make good use of all gifts, without depending upon them. And without intelligence, gold, repute, beauty, the wonderful gifts of Tyche can act like poison and eventually destroy us. For the gifts of Tyche are external advantages, and undeserved good Fortune can become a source of misery for the ungrateful, selfish, and greedy types.

The gift of Tyche's feminine wisdom helps us to understand that oftentimes in life we do not have control, that moving with, not against, the natural ebb and flow challenges us to let go of the outer world's need for lust and desires with perfect outcomes.

Tyche leads us into the Fortunes of the inner life, where we can observe the challenges that necessitate sudden movement and change, which can actually lead us to better Fortune than previously thought possible. What is essential in her wisdom is that the changing circumstances are embraced as being right and perfect regardless of whether they appear advantageous or as adversities. This is often hard to do when you have deadlines to meet and outcomes to create on schedule. She teaches us that our Fortunes are always shifting and never stagnant, perhaps without our choosing, and that it's in this magic dance of life that the fates help to co-create with the divine. The key of which is in the total surrender of things and hidden in the wisdom of "let go, let god or Goddess actually".

Many say it's what lies outside the sphere of moral purpose, which cannot be possessed by mankind, and therefore everything should be surrendered to the real owner, who is Tyche the Goddess of the fates of Fortune. Surrendering all to her is the only way to have peace and accept that 'whatever will be, will be'.

Goddess of Passion
Pele

Pele is a Hawaiian Volcano and Fire Goddess. She is known as one Who Shapes the Sacred Land. Pele is the Volcano, the expression and embodiment of the Divine Creative Feminine Power. She is the Flame of Passion and the Fire of Purpose, She is the Energy of Dynamic Action and She is the core Glowing Essence of Eternal and Profound Love.

Pele's energy teaches us that when we know who we are and when we honour that energy, when we honour our True Self we will find our place in the world. She reminds us that when we are pursuing our True Path, to persevere despite perceived obstacles. We are encouraged to not give up before we reach the destination of our dreams. Her forms are many, including the volcano, lava, and fire/flame. Goddess Pele also has ability to shape-shift and will show herself as a beautiful young woman, as a crone and as a white dog.

Aligned with Volcanoes, Pele is sometimes associated with destruction and violence. Goddesses associated with destruction are often misunderstood and perhaps even misjudged. When working with the Divine Feminine, destruction often equates to clearing away that which no longer serves us and may be considered part of the cycle of birth, death and rebirth. In actuality, Goddess Pele's Volcanoes are more of a creative force, creating and shaping land, clearing the old and laying the foundation for new. Through this Volcanic activity Pele shapes the land, as her lava spews forth she gives birth to the islands and may be considered a life giving Mother Goddess. As one who shapes the land, Pele reminds us of our own dynamic creative power. We are reminded that we constantly create and shape our own life with the powerful energy that we project through our thoughts, our words, our emotions, our beliefs and intentions and through our imagination. Through this awareness we are able to take responsibility, wielding our creative power with clear focus and with positive intention. In this way, we can create exactly what we desire and wish to experience.

Goddess Pele is an extremely dynamic Divine Feminine Force. She sets fire to the falsehoods that women are weak and incapable and that to be feminine means to be fragile and helpless. Pele demonstrates exquisite feminine beauty combined with unquestionable capability, steadfast strength, dignity and divine power. This awesome aspect of the Lady, loves and lives with profound passion, providing a platform for both women and men to transcend illusions related to feminine power.

Pele also helps us communicate honestly and to set appropriate boundaries when necessary. Pele brings confidence, courage and promotes positive action. Goddess Pele helps us clear the illusions that we are incapable and helps us to realign with our Divine Truth so that we may realise our True Potential.

Feeling fatigued or burned out? Since this Fire Goddess is aligned with Energy, upon our request, she will help us to remember our eternal connection to the Divine Flame, refueling and re-energising our body, mind and spirit with Divine Energy. Physical energy, motivation, empowerment and strength can be found with the Element of Fire. Since Fire is a fantastic source of Energy, the Fire Element lends awesome fuel for manifestation, helping to lend power to our positive intentions. Pele will guide us to utilise our Fire power wisely, helping us to avoid burning our candle at both ends, realising that regular rest and proper self-care are a necessary aspect of the refueling process.

Fire Power is Goddess Pele's Gift. The Fire Element brings Energy! The Element of Fire also has a tremendous force to transmute and clear old, stagnate energy. The Fire Element can be invoked for protection, creating an energetic field of protective and transmutive energy.

Through honouring our own eternal Flame and inner fires and by realising our innate and eternal connection to this Divine Goddess' Energy, we will naturally start to feel alive with vital, vibrant energy, be naturally enthusiastic and empowered by her presence.

Goddess of Compassion

Kuan Yin

Compassion – "Release judgments about yourself and others, instead focus on the love and light that is within everyone".

Kuan Yin is one of the most beloved and popular Eastern divinities, and is the essence of purity, nurturing love, and gentle power. She is a physically and spiritually beautiful Chinese goddess of mercy, compassion and protection. Her name means "she who hears prayers". It is said that Kuan Yin does in fact hear and answer every prayer sent her way.

Kuan Yin is considered both a Goddess and a bodhisattva or "enlightened being". Bodhisattvas can become Buddha's however, Kuan Yin had such a deep love of humanity that after she attained enlightenment, instead of ascending to Buddhahood, she chose to remain in human form until everyone of us becomes enlightened. She is devoted to helping us fully open up to our spiritual gifts; attain profound knowledge and enlightenment, to reduce world suffering. It's said that the mere uttering of her name affords guaranteed protection from harm.

Kuan Yin is often called "the Mother Mary of the East" because she represents feminine divinity and Goddess energy in the Buddhist religion, in the same way that Mary radiates sweet loving femininity within Christianity. Kuan Yin teaches us to practice a life of harmlessness, using great care to ease suffering in the world and not to add to it in anyway.

KuanYin's energy depicts Gentleness as the strength behind true power. It comes from feeding yourself with nourishing words, thoughts, deeds, intentions and all forms of food. She helps us to attract only kind and gentle life lessons and relationships. She helps us to transform harshness into gentleness by refusing to see anything but the shining light that's within each person and situation. This intention begins with your relationship with yourself. Learn to be gentle with and kind to yourself in all ways. Be happy; be kind, be sweet, but most of all be true to yourself. Make it okay to have rest and recoup after times of challenge or crisis. Give yourself permission to be still, to gather yourself up and come to yourself in your own time.

As a result of this, her energy acts as a deep transformational healer, releasing pent up feelings of guilt or shame and replacing them with self-acceptance and forgiveness. Great peace is the gift of self acceptance, which lets go of struggle and resistance.

Her messages to us simple yet profound: Don't be so hard on yourself or others. Release the need for perfectionist tendencies. Avoid gossip or bad-mouthing of yourself or others. Keep your thoughts pure about yourself and others by remaining open to see the good in all things and deeds, remaining positive. She offers protection especially for women and children. She helps awaken musical interests and gifts as well as spiritual and psychic abilities. Through connecting with her compassion many are healed form a deep sense of acceptance that life is the way it is and that its okay. She allows the turmoil within others to remain with them so they can figure it out without judgement.

No other figure has held such an important place in popular worship as Kuan Yin. Her image can be found in most homes, temples and shrines everywhere throughout the East. Many believe she was originally an ancient Chinese princess called Miaoshan. There is an ancient legend of how this pure and holy princess became known as Guanyin; the merciful, compassionate protectress of mortals becoming known as queen of the sea.

Goddess of Truth, Wisdom & Justice
Athena

Wisdom, Justice, Truth
Stop procrastinating, trust your truth and listen to it's inner wisdom by taking positive action towards your success.

In ancient Greek mythology Athena has a colourful and mysterious past full of intrigue. Stories of her origin were tainted when she defeated Poseidon in a contest for the main city. The city took her name and became known as Athens, city of the Goddess. Men of the day outwardly accepted the results of the contest, however they fought back by making up a story about her motherless birth being from the head of the chief god Zeus, delivered fully mature as a warrior ready for battle, wearing gold armour. They also struck back at women by passing three new laws: women were barred from voting, their citizenship was stripped, and children were given the father's name, not the mother's. Making Athena born only of the father, apparently devoid of a mother, was an attempt to eradicate matriarchy. However she came by her fierce masculine (appearing) countenance, Athena apparently never consorted with men, remaining forever a virgin.

This mythology reflects how the Athena archetype is often identified as being a proud daughter, born of a powerful, wise and loving father. In this way she knew only her father's logical and rational ways, often admiring and preferring the company of men. This Goddess is then powerful in her identification with all things worldly and masculine; the mind and its intelligence, the ability to take positive action when putting thoughts into form.

We can easily spot the women who identify with the Athena archetype. They are strong willed and are typically found in accounting, law and politics, management and business, or governmental roles, able to easily navigate the day-to-day red tape of our authoritarian institutions. Athena represents the wise 'Amazonian' warrior Goddess, whose qualities engage the clever and intelligent female thinkers in our modern society who are born leaders, teachers and trainers, unafraid of challenge. This type of women prefers to be in charge. She likes and needs the challenge of her own business or prefers to work as an executive in the corporate sector; she is focused and disciplined, able to manage a home and family whilst making strategic financial decisions. These women are formidable and able to comfortably meet men on a mental level, holding their own intellectually whilst feeling safe in their feminine identity.

Athena is most vividly symbolised by the snake, seen in the famous statue in her main temple, which rears up beside her, taller than any human viewer. The snake gives her the wisdom of insight, the ability to shed skins and let go, and therefore make adjustments and changes whilst using intuitive abilities to see with clarity. Frequently sculptured wearing gold armour and a helmet, carrying a shield or spear, these are her warrior symbols of fearless battle. With right action she is able to conquer any obstacles placed on her pathway at will. The most captivating of her symbols is that of the owl, which appears in early Athenian art forms sitting on the Goddess's shoulder. She harnessed the owl's ability to observe its prey, to silently pierce the darkness, to see that which is hidden. It gave her a powerful dual mental capability of uncovering the subconscious possibilities, giving her insight into future outcomes. In this way, she could be her own devil's advocate, enabling wiser decisions. The owl represents all that is mindful and truthful, an oracle-like wisdom, helping to form a wise balance of will and integrity. This mental agility enables her to steer a better course of action, making her an astute life strategist. Also, the Greek columns are an ever-present symbol of her connection to the male, father, governing authoritarian systems of state, resulting in the Parthenon, the "Virgin Temple", being made her shrine.

If you already identify with or need Athena's qualities to be activated, enhanced or brought into your life, then call upon her wisdom and clarity, for she is an amazing force to be reckoned with on many levels. She will help you to find that balance between your chosen profession and love life, work and family, as well as aiding you in your career pursuits or academic and intellectual needs, and of course all aspects regarding the running of your own type of successful business.

For a long time her qualities have been at the forefront, helping women to step more easily into their own power, once again claiming and taking their rightful place alongside that of men, helping to bring into balance the masculine and feminine.

Goddess of the Home & Hearth

Hestia

Hestia, mistress of the hearth, holder of the flame and shelter of the earth, is one of the oldest goddesses among the most ancient of beings. Her name means hearth, which was the central fire of the home and possibly the oldest recognised symbol for unifying the human race. A town or city is only an extended family, and therefore had its sacred hearth where everyone gathered - symbolising a harmonious community of citizens and common worship. The hearth was looked upon as the sacred centre of domestic life, and so Hestia was the central goddess of domestic life and the giver of all domestic happiness and blessings, and as such she was believed to dwell in the inner part of every house. If you moved to another land to live, you would take part of the sacred fire from where you came to set up a new hearth. Birthright was honoured and cultural roots were therefore sustained, and worshipped at the fire. As the hearth of a house was also seen as the altar on which sacrifices were offered to the domestic gods, Hestia was looked upon as presiding over all sacrifices, and, as the goddess of the sacred fire of the altar, she had a share in the sacrifices in all the temples of the gods. When sacrifices were offered, she was invoked first, and the first part of any sacrifice was offered to her. These sacrifices consisted often of fruit, water, oil, wine and one year old cows.

Hestia was said to be the first-born child of Kronos and Rhea – and was swallowed by her father at birth. Zeus than forced the old Titan father to disgorge Hestia and her siblings.

Hestia was the first to teach the domestic arts to the human race, presiding over the cooking of bread and the preparation of the family meals, and included teaching mankind to build houses. There were only a few special temples for Hestia in Greece, because every prytaneum was a sanctuary of the goddess.

In the home of the gods, Mt Olympus, Hestia tended the sacred fire that opened all of their councils. She was known to keep the civic hearth, and also kept peace and harmony on more than one occasion. The temple fire was central to all ritual, becoming a sanctuary, and a place where the ancestral spirits where worshipped. Pythagoras once said that the fire of Hestia was the centre of the earth and the womb of the world. For every being of all life is nurtured, sustained and warmed because of the fire molten core of mother earth, and perhaps we should recall this fact occasionally and be filled with gratitude.

If you are a homebody or a domestic goddess with a strong sense of place or family then you are already a devotee of the goddess Hestia. You can call upon her to help you to connect to that part that needs to feel at home, that needs to feel grounded in domesticity with love for the joyousness and comfort it brings. Hestia can help find the perfect home and helps you feel the connection to a place.

Hestia offers you natural guidance as you commune in a caring and sensitive manner, mindful that everyone is different and deserves respect and nurturing. No matter what, she ensures we gather as a sacred family who cares for each other, listens to each other and forgives each other.

We can call upon her to protect those we love, our friends and especially our family. She helps us to honour our peers and wise ones from our ancient ancestors and is concerned with the politics of the time and decisions that are made for the betterment of all. Hestia is a very real and grounded goddess who sits comfortably on the earth and helps us to acknowledge our living environment, honouring our personal space and those we commune and share it with. She is a heart warming peaceful goddess, who serves with love through the flames that would warm and enliven our hearts passions for life, and all those who share in our journey of sacred togetherness, clan and family.

Goddess of the Underworld Persephone

Hope, Growth, Renewal
Climb out of the darkness & into the light of new hope, Spring brings the promise of fresh new growth & renewal.

Persephone, a young Greek goddess, was also known in her childhood by the name Kore (or Cora - meaning young maiden). She was the only child of the union between Demeter (goddess of the bountiful harvest) and Zeus, the mighty king of the Olympians. Persephone was said to have an idyllic childhood; her nurturing and doting mother raised her and she played joyfully with her father's other daughters, the Greek goddesses Athena and Aphrodite. Always a cheerful and compliant child, the little goddess Persephone was not only a parent's dream, but was extremely beautiful.

While still a young maiden Hades, king of the underworld, abducted her after he had negotiated for her hand in marriage with Zeus. Demeter was distraught and, fuelled with grief, she stopped her blessings on the earth which became barren. After much pleading with Zeus, she visited her daughter in the underworld, only to realise that Persephone could not return permanently to the surface. So a bargain was struck to allow both mother and daughter to visit each other. Persephone was allowed to stay with Hades in the underworld for four months each year (winter) and would return to the earth and her mother for the remaining eight months. Each year, as Persephone left to join her husband in the underworld, it was said Demeter would grieve and bring on the cold, barren winters. But a few months later Persephone, the goddess associated with awakening, would return to bring spring and its verdant growth in her wake - thus establishing the seasons. Persephone represents both the youthful, innocent, and joyous maiden aspect of womanhood, as well as the more womanly self who, after losing her innocence and loosening family attachments, began to consciously choose her path for herself. Letting go of overbearing or doting parents is difficult but must be done if one is to become an adult.

Persephone is also goddess of the soul - possessing it's dark and frightening wisdom (held in the underworld), which many avoid facing within themselves. As a psychotherapist I have often used this mythology when explaining the need for depression and what we learn from its depths and wisdom. Often we retrieve aspects of the deeper self when in this state and many avoid feelings of grief - but rest assured it is a great teacher to us. Persephone is also the harbinger of spring as she rises each year to help her mother Demeter with the pollination of all trees, fruits, flowers and crops upon Earth. She is also a reminder of all the new growth and abundance that the hope of the bright green growth Spring brings. This is when Persephone comes up from the underworld to be with her mother Demeter, to melt the winter chill with her warmth, help her with the planting of new seeds and tend the gardens of Earth. It's a time of renewal, of fairy magic, of butterflies dancing, bees buzzing and flowers opening up. It is a time full of promise and hope when blossom buds form the beginning of fruits, soon to be harvested when ripe in the coming summer. Persephone's youthfulness graces our hearts with love.

Spring is the return of all things youthful, it's a happy time when the heart is light and the promise of new beginnings is available. It's a great time to clean out the old and let the new light into our lives, relationships, businesses and homes. A time to honour the journey thus far with a view as to what possibilities it can now grow and expand from. New seeds fill a fertile open mind and so the taking on of new studies or creative ventures is worth exploring. In this energy there are endless possibilities as to the planting of new thoughts, concepts, ideas, new projects, business ventures and travels. It is a time to open up to the new and to leave behind the old and start fresh. Many marriages and ceremonies are performed in spring, as it's a great fertile time to procreate and start new life. The fruits of abundance are visible evidence, available as proof to us all, that things can be renewed. The seasons remind us of the cycles of life, that nothing stays the same and that all things pass. That renewal is possible as new things begin to take form.

Warrior Goddess of strength
Brigit

The goddess Brigid is a traditional Celtic goddess, known to be a patroness of healing, the hearth, of bardic poetry and a keeper of the blacksmith craft - which are all practical and inspired wisdoms. The blacksmith was seen as a sacred trust and was associated with magickal powers since it involved mastering the primal element of fire. The alchemical moulding of metal took great skill, acquired through knowledge and strength. As a solar deity her attributes are of one who is blessed by the heavenly flames, often called the Bright One, she inspires all skills associated with the element of fire. Although she is not actually identified with the physical sun, she is certainly the benefactress of transformational forces, inner healing and all the vital life force energy that fire involves.

Bards would invoke her protection from vengence of the ones whom illuminated their tales. She was seen as looking after the seer-poets, helping to preserve their poetic function by keeping the oral traditions alive. It is widely believed that those poets who have gone before inhabit the realms between the worlds, overlapping into ours so that the old songs and stories will be heard and repeated. Many of these oral traditions were never written until much later, but are still taught and can be heard orally by certain storytellers today.

In Druid mythology, the infant goddess was fed with milk from a sacred cow from the otherworld. Brigid owned an apple orchard in the Otherworld and her bees would bring their magical nectar back to earth. The apple then became spiritually synonymous with the Druids. It is said that wherever she walked, small flowers and shamrocks would appear. As a fire goddess her gifts were that of light (knowledge), inspiration, and the vital and healing energy of the sun. As the bringer of hope and inspiration, her strength was so great within the Celtic lands that her shrines and sacred wells survived the conversion to Christianity, upon where she was canonised as Saint Brigit of Kildare (Ireland) and Bride in Scotland. As a result the Celtic cross, the cauldron, all wells, and the hearth of poor people became sacred Celtic symbols attributed to her. Her many followers were known to keep continuous lamps alight at her shrines, symbolising how Brigid's light warms us and lights our way, sustaining the light within us through our difficult times. However, her fame spread quickly throughout Europe and she became revered almost everywhere.

Brigid is known in many forms and in many cultures now and often is seen as one of the great mothers. It is said she was present as a midwife at the birth of the Christ. She loved animals and is associated with sheep and cows and milk (the sustenance of the mother energy). As a result she shows us that we must learn to allow ourselves to mother ourselves if we feel neglected and give nurturing when we need it. Often women forget to do this to themselves, but have no trouble giving to others they love or care for. She teaches us as women to give back to ourselves, learning how to receive her energy as we bathe in own mothering love.

Her mothering, healing energy warms our heart and makes us feel like we belong, its nurturing timelessness has a gentle transformational healing effect that lightens a troubled heart or mind. Her comfortable warmth enwraps us like the glow from a warm fire's flame on a chilly winters night. Call upon her as you bask in the flames soaking up their warmth and ask her to inspire your creative urges, and light your pathway ahead.

Brigid asks you to drink from the healing waters of the earth and understand the depth of your being as it stirs within - be open to her wisdom and strength and let inspiration and the promise of hope fill your dreams. Let her nurturing power and inner vitality heal any apathy and sadness within. Let the flames dance a primordial jig in your heart as you share the music of your souls love with the hearts of others.

Goddess of Flowers
Cordelia

Play Outdoors, Friendships
Create balance within your lifestyle, go outside and enjoy sports, being with friends or mother nature.

Known as the Welsh Goddess of summer flowers, Cordelia is honoured as being the Queen of May and of the fairies. Seen as an important Goddess, bridging the gap between seasons. She was a strong maiden Goddess Archetype, having been the target of ardent attention from suitors competing to win her love. Daughter of the sea god Llyr. Connected with Beltane and often called the May Queen. In her myths there was a famous rivalry of the Gods Gwyn and Gwyrthur over her each Samhain and Bealtaine. This is one of the origins of the Holly King and Oak King duel, which is commemorated each Yule and Midsummer in most Celtic traditions...

The myth goes something like this:
The Holly King, the Lord of the Winterwood and darksome twin of the waning year, rules from Midsummer to Midwinter. At Midsummer, he goes to battle with his twin, the Oak King, for the favor of the Goddess. He slays the Oak King, who goes to rest in Caer Arianrhod until they do battle again at Midsummer. The Oak King and Holly King are mortal enemies at Midsummer and Midwinter, but they are two sides of a whole. Neither could exist without the other. There are two themes which run throughout the Holly King and Oak King saga. The first, of course, is the two great yearly battles between the two. The second is the sacrificial mating, death, and resurrection of each in his season. At Lammas, the peak of the Holly King's reign, he sacrificially mates with the Great Mother, dies in her embrace, and is resurrected. This is an enactment of the natural fertility theme of the season, and is not uncommon in other mythologies: Osiris, Tammuz, Dionysus, Balder, and Jesus are only a few other gods who die and are

resurrected. (The Oak King on the other hand, mates, dies and is resurrected at Beltane.) This aspect of the Holly King and Oak King is not widely discussed, but is an important element in their roles as fertility gods.]

Cordelia defied her sea god father's wishes, to marry the man of her choice, and became the inspiration for Cordelia in Shakespeare's King Lear.
Her Modern Archetypal Message: In standing in her power whilst defying her sea god father's wishes, her inner strength brought us a time honoured message; that despite her light, happy and abundant life giving feminine disposition, good fortune can be ours, if we make up our mind and stand firm in our choices. That to 'Do what you know to be right for you,' is important in becoming and remaining an individual. That learning to be true to oneself is a must for everyone not just females. Gone are the days where we should constantly give our power away to others, by always being told what to do. Whether it's well meaning parents or friends, sharing opinions about how they think you should live your life, it's important to know that you can face these pressures and all of life's challenges and adversities.

Cordelia teaches us all that even though we can feel fragile and look gentle and submissive we don't have act like it. That to hold our ground and face our fears is important. As the Goddess of flowers her message is telling us to go outside and play in nature more often… to go smell the flowers. Call upon Cordelia whenever you feel stressed or trapped indoors. You can "escape" from office routines by closing your eyes and imagining yourself standing in a field of flowers with her during a perfect springtime afternoon. Make time and create balance by going outdoors and spending time with nature.
Place bright coloured flowers around your desk or where ever you work and keep nature close as a reminder of the great 'Mother Goddess' for she is always with us, but it's nice to see her face.

Goddess of Purification
White Tara

White Tara is an emanation or aspect of Tara a female Buddha and Hindu Mother Goddess, the creator of all life. Tara is the many faces of the female Buddha, and is represented by many colours. The white Tara represents purity of life and is therefore connected with longevity. One calls on her for health, strength, and longevity. But it is her inner purity and sensitive nature that she is most recognized for. Her white colour indicates this purity, but also indicates that she is Truth complete and undifferentiated compassion in action. Her sensitivity allows her to see all suffering and hear all cries for help, even in the human world, even in the worlds of pain, using both ordinary and psychic or extraordinary means of perception.

As a result she demonstrates that to become open, to be receptive to truth one must rid oneself of all that is impure, all that is of the ego, and become sensitive to all that is visible. To put up walls and create barriers is to operate in fear, needing protection for false cause. That when ones heart and mind is of pure intent then no harm can come to you. That to be truly gifted in seeing one must become sensitive to all things, remove all veils that would cloud ones inner perception. Often our lives and our body can become toxic through low or negative energies, food and thoughts.

Her message is to aid your growth by purifying your mental, emotional and physical bodies so that your spiritual selves may step forward in ascension. This will unblock your psychic awareness centre (third eye) and help develop you more spiritually. Peel away the false things and gratifications that bring only emotional comfort to the pleasure senses and base egos needs.

That to be mature and grow we have to be able to be truly in the world to see it fully and not constantly want to dull the senses. Letting go of toxic foods, chemicals, relationships, situations, loud noise, crowds and violent media will protect and honour your sensitivity. These are your spiritual gifts and need to be respected and treated kindly.

The White Tara is represented as a mature woman, full breasted and wise woman, someone that cares about humanity that nurtures the hurts of life away. Don't be afraid to use her healing qualities, they can be very powerful if called upon. Spend time connecting with her, allow her to enter you mind and purify your thinking, to lift you out of negative emotional dramas.

She will hear your prayers and answer them; she will act on your behalf. Such is the depth of caring and compassion of the White Tara.

White Tara helps us with our longer-term problems, particularly problems of physical or mental/emotional health. It sometimes seems as if she is more aloof or distant, harder to contact at first. Then it is as if she sends us healing energies and mystical power and understandings. The Rainbow Body practice is also identified with White Tara, (*some also consider her to be connected to the Lotus family*).

Other Books & Oracles by the Author

Modern Goddess Oracle
60 Cards & Guidebook

REIKI a Transformational
Spiritual Healing Path

Blue Moon Oracle
52 Cards & Guidebook

The Art of Meaningful Living
Simple Wisdom for the 21st Century

The Third EYE
Psychic Secrets for the Mystics

S'Roya Rose TAROT
Cards & Guidebook

In Search of SOUL
Who am I? Why am I here?
What's my purpose?

CHAKRAS
& Their Hidden Wisdom

TAROT A Sacred Doorway
A must have Tarot Compendium
for the modern Cosmic Sage

*For more information on,
or to stock or purchase any of
S'Roya's book titles or oracle
cards tarot decks or magazines,
please email her on:
email@sroyarose.com
or visit her website:
www.sroyarose.com
or alternatively visit
www.phoenixdistribution.com.au*

About S'Roya Rose

S'Roya is a gifted clairvoyant Psycho Therapist, and well known Australian Celebrity Psychic Medium, she is an initiating High Priestess of the Goddess, who works with the angelic, elemental, Ascended Masters, ancient Mystics, the Animal clans, and other cosmic Shamanic realms, able to connect with spirit guides and deceased loved ones.

Having appeared nationally on channel Seven's 'New Age of Aquarius' show, and on channel nine's 'Sunday Show', she also makes guest appearances on Psychic TV OZ. She has been teaching Reiki and the Tarot, facilitating Spiritual and Psychic development workshops and running Goddess and psychic circles for 18 years.

An accomplished writer, she's has been active in shifting consciousness publishing various book titles having been the creatrix and editor of many spiritual magazines ie; Deja Vu, Dharma, BlackRose, Goddess Guru & Avalon. Recently she launched her amazing Modern Goddess Oracle deck and her latest fabulous Blue Moon Oracle wisdom cards.

A natural born Mystic of the modern age she is respected as being a wise goddess, her counsel being constantly sought after, usually bookings must be made weeks in advance. To book a personal session, via Skype or Phone Reading with S'Roya or a Healing Psycho Therapy session, simply email her on:

email@sroyarose.com ~ www.sroyarose.com

www.ingramcontent.com/pod-product-compliance
Lightning Source LLC
Chambersburg PA
CBHW070919160426
43193CB00011B/1526